EAT MY MEAT

A BEGINNERS FIELD DRESSING GUIDE FOR SMALL GAME

PAT GATZ

CONTENTS

A Special Gift To Our Readers!

Included with your purchase of this book is our Field Dressing Starters Guide. This guide will prepare you with some essential critical tips not to forget when you start field dressing small game. It has a secret golden nugget at the end, too!

Click the link below and let us know which email address to deliver it to.

www.patgatz.com

INTRODUCTION

Hunting can be incredibly satisfying when you're experienced. You get the thrill of the hunt, followed by the immense satisfaction that you've been able to catch something that is going to provide sustenance for you and your family. While we rarely eat the skins of our catches, they can be useful for other purposes. However, if you've never hunted and dressed your kills, you might feel entirely overwhelmed by the prospect of doing so. You may feel lost, confused, and may even make some mistakes that will render your kill inedible. Of course, to dress a kill in the field will require practice that you can only get in a hands-on environment.

I was born in Northern Ontario. My home was surrounded by thick forest and marshes that were ripe with many animals for the taking. Ever since the tender age of three, I've been taught the basics of hunting. I grew up raised by wolves—or at least, it felt like it with my siblings running wild. I began with a little slingshot, shooting at snakes, partridge, and any other small game I could land a hit on. Hunting flows through my blood.

I've spent over 20 years out in nature, learning what the beautiful Mother Earth offers us. Sure, I could live in a city, surrounded by everything I need just a few clicks of the internet away, but is that living? I don't think so. For me, true happiness is the exhilaration of providing for myself. It is to be out in nature and see that we all are interconnected. We hunt, we eat, we live. Animals are born, they die, they return to the earth. The circle of life might make some uncomfortable, but to me, it makes every moment of living that much more desirable. It makes every moment of my life feel like an adventure, truly cherished because you never know what day will be your last.

Over the years, I've had plenty of time to learn about hunting and field dressing my meat. I've practiced and perfected my technique. And now, it's time that I take my expertise and pass it on to the next generation. Hunting is a sport that everyone should learn to appreciate—after all, not too long ago, our ancestors had to go out and kill their food on their own. Grocery stores don't exist in the state of nature. Be self-sufficient to survive in a natural world, and that's where hunting and dressing come into play.

You might be surprised to discover that hunting isn't necessarily the hardest part of the process. To kill an animal is relatively easy. However, to clean it and prepare it for consumption takes much more finesse than simply shooting something. As you read through my guide, you're going to be introduced to information that will help you become a professional field dresser. This is the information that I wish I had when I first began hunting—it would have saved me from wasting time and valuable meat.

Nowadays, I love field dressing, but I also understand that so many people are squeamish about the entire process. That's why I've made this guide as easy to follow as possible for beginners: This is supposed to be the beginner's holy grail about everything that you need to know before you ever step foot out into the wilderness. By the end of this, you'll have the technical knowledge—then, all you're missing is the practice to master it.

If you're unsure what I mean about field dressing, don't worry too much about it. Simply put, field dressing involves removing the animal's internal organs to avoid decay and improve the general quality of the meat. It comes with several critical benefits that will help you ensure that you stay healthy when eating meat that isn't prepared professionally.

1. **Preventing bacterial growth**: It helps you avoid the growth of bacteria on the carcass, therefore ensuring that the meat stays fresh until it is adequately preserved. If the meat is left without field dressing, it can decay quickly. The act of field dressing helps cool the meat, lowering the body temperature of the meat to prevent it from remaining in the danger zone too long.

2. **Ease of transportation**: Field dressing makes it very easy to move your game from the field to your home because you've already removed

the guts and other parts of the animal that you will not be using or consuming. Especially for larger game, such as deer, this could be the difference between carrying it or not.

3. **It gets you the full hunter's experience**: Your hunting experience is incomplete if you have not dressed the animal yourself. You will enjoy the whole experience when you field dress an animal you hunted. This allows you to understand the completeness of the process and to have all credit for the meat.

As you read this book, you'll discover the most critical aspects of dressing and field dressing for minor games. It assumes that you're a total novice to field dressing and that everything you'll be learning is brand new. We'll be covering several popular small game animals that can be found in North America.

If you are just like me that have a knack for small game, then know that I put this material together with you in mind to make it easy for you to handle your small game meat. Hunting is what I do and love. After studying this field guide, easily field dress your small game, butcher it and package it later. You can expect to find information such as:

- How to carry out field dressing
- Steps to take to the field to help you dress small game animals are explicitly found in North America.
- Effective transporting techniques to take your small game home in such a way that the meat maintains its freshness and quality.
- How to Hang, cool, and age your meat for the best tasting.
- How to butcher your meat and butchering methods.
- Cooking your small game and secret recipes.

Are you ready to prepare yourself for the next step in becoming self-sufficient? There's no better time than the present to get started. Why wait one day longer? Be ready to process your next kill. It's not as hard as so many people make it out to be once you've tried.

1

BASIC GEAR, TOOLS, AND EQUIPMENT FOR BEGINNERS

Before you rush out to hunt with just your weapon of choice, consider that there are many, many pieces of equipment that you probably want to have on hand. This will vary from whether you wish to hunt small game small or big game. You'll need to kill, process, and store your game, and you'll also need some general safety supplies on hand just in case you need them.

Your tools are essential to your success as you hunt and field dress the game you have. You need to be prepared to keep yourself comfortable as well. Finding the fine line between having everything you're going to need and being able to carry it all can be a bit of a balancing act, but the more you work on finding that perfect combination of what you should have on hand and what you should do while out and about.

ESSENTIAL STORAGE AND TRANSPORTATION EQUIPMENT

Going to the field without the right equipment is a waste of your time. You want to be sure that you are prepared to execute a clean and proper field dressing, so you don't kill your game in vain and so you can ensure that you are safe throughout the process. Many diseases could pass from animal to hunter during your interaction with wild game, and many steps could pose a challenge if you try to prepare your game without all the proper supplies.

☰ BACKPACK

An essential item that helps you to keep everything else organized. Your backpack serves as your one-stop shop for everything that you'll need during your time hunting. It should be large enough that you're able to fit everything you'll need, but also not too large or heavy, so it doesn't impede your movement as you hunt.

If you're not interested in a backpack, using even a game vest or fanny pack can also provide you with a valid option. As long as it fits all of your supplies and tools, any sort of storage will work.

☰ GAME BAGS

If you want to keep your meat clean, one of the best ways to do so is to ensure that you've got a game bag. You can put your meat right into the game bag before you take the meat to the butcher elsewhere, or you can also put dressed animals right into the bag to prevent maggots from flies landing on the meat, as well as to cool the meat. Game bags are breathable enough to let the remnants of body heat escape without letting in bugs. These come in many materials, such as cotton, synthetic, or even trash bags. Plastic bags can be used in a pinch, but the meat won't breathe unless you leave it open, which leads to problems with bugs contaminating the meat.

☰ TRASH BAGS

If you've got a lot of waste that you don't want to leave out in the wild for Mother Nature to take care of, you can always pack along a trash bag for all of your garbage. In a pinch, a trash bag has a lot of great purposes, from being able to create a barrier between your meat and the ground while you field dress it, to being a rain jacket if a sudden storm passes by, and even used as a game bag in a pinch, though this is usually not recommended.

HARNESS AND SLED

If you intend to kill many animals at once, you might also consider getting yourself a sled and harness. Keeping a harness in your toolbox when going hunting will make it easy for you to come back with less frustration after a day out in the fields. If you would have to drag your hunt to your car, you will need to use a harness to distribute the weight of the animals evenly on you so that you can carry it easily. A sled could also help you transport your meat after field dressing in a snowy part of town.

ICE CHEST

If you can do so, it's a good idea to have an ice chest accessible during your hunting trip. Whether you set up a camp or have a home base set up in your car, knowing that you have ice means that you don't have to rush home as soon as you get the kill. You can leave your processed game to chill while you continue to hunt. Chilling the meat is essential to prevent it from spoiling too quickly.

ESSENTIAL FIELD DRESSING, SKINNING, AND BUTCHERING EQUIPMENT

When it's time for you to skin, field dress, and butcher your game, you'll want to go into it with several supplies that you'll be able to use to make the process easier. While you could probably get by with any old knife and your hands sometimes, you'll probably want to have some equipment on hand so you can get through the process easier and keep things cleaner. Remember, cleanliness is essential if you're going to eat the food you've hunted with a low risk of illness. Keeping the meat clean is often the best prevention, and that cleanliness starts in butchering your meat the right way.

BOWL

Before you begin, an important consideration is to ensure that you have some sort of bowl and container that you can use for the meat. Since we're talking about small game here, be able to take a plain stainless steel bowl that will fit just fine for all but the largest game. This prevents you from placing your kill on the ground while opening it up to remove the entrails.

GLOVES

It's important to use gloves for your field dressing for sanitary purposes. The gloves should be elbow length so that it shields your arms from any contamination. Try to sanitize your hands before putting on your gloves, and if you're frequently in areas where water access is difficult, consider getting disposable gloves. I prefer using gloves made from latex material or one with a latex feel for better grip and fitting.

SHARP KNIVES

A sharp knife is an essential tool for field dressing; you'll want at least two of them, with one heavier and the other smaller to cut through delicate organs. You may even want to consider keeping a small sharpener with you if any of your knives aren't up to par with what you'd like.

BONE SAW

Depending on what you're hunting, carry a bone saw as well. This will make it easier to cut through tough bones, especially if you get ambitious and go for a deer if the opportunity arises. This shouldn't be a problem for most small game, but if you have a large rabbit or goose, you might use one if you can't quite get the leverage. It could be good just in case, too. It's always better to be prepared, and these aren't too heavy.

HEADLAMP

Just in case it isn't one of those lucky days where you shoot an animal in the early hours. If the evening comes down on you while you are trying to field dress your meat, be well prepared by having your headlamp with you. You should get a headlamp with powerful battery life and designed for mountaineers so that it fits into your backpack and get one that is sturdy and can be firmly placed on the head, and even in cases of a slight fall it can work perfectly.

☰ CLEAN RAGS AND PAPER TOWELS

Messes happen in the best of times. This can be a huge problem when you're in the middle of the forest without access to clean running water. At the very least, you can use rags and paper towels to blot up the mess or perhaps pour a bit of your bottled water onto it to use as a sort of wet cloth. Try keeping these within a sealed plastic bag, so they stay nice and clean until you need them.

2

TRANSPORTATION AND STORAGE

After you've hunted and cleaned your harvest, you've done just half the work. Unless you're going to slap that meat onto a campfire and enjoy it nearly immediately, you must take the time to transport the meat appropriately. That meat, once processed, needs to be made into a cooler or refrigerator as soon as possible. This is especially true if you're hunting in the heat of summer. It may not be *as* important amid winter, depending upon where you are hunting and what the temperatures in the area are like, but it's a good idea to ensure that your meat is somewhere cool as soon as possible.

With small game, you're already at an advantage compared to people trying to bring home some other large harvest. You're lucky in the sense that the meat that you collect can be stored in a cooler or some other easily transported case that can help keep it cool.

The most important thing to remember is that if you're ever in doubt about whether your meat is safe to eat, it's better to dispose of it than risk eating it anyway to prevent the transmission of disease. However, there are many ways that you can take care of your harvests to keep them safe and ready to eat.

As you read through this chapter, you will be introduced to three important aspects of hunting. First, we'll address what to do to clean up your kill site. Then, we'll go over how to store the meat safely so you know you can enjoy it when you get home. Finally, we will discuss how to transport it home safely to be confident that you did nothing that might contaminate the meat.

≡ BEFORE YOU LEAVE THE KILL SITE

Upon killing small game, it's essential to get it cleaned as quickly as possible to prevent it from causing problems later on. The entrails swell up and may even burst within the animal's abdomen, which can cause you many issues. Alternatively, if you pierced the intestines or stomach, the leakage can cause the meat to spoil, and that spoilage can happen rapidly if the weather is warmer.

However, it's considered in poor taste to leave behind scraps. Most people don't care to find piles of entrails, scraps, and bones that you've left behind. Thankfully, with small game, the entrails are much smaller than if you had hunted, say, a deer, but you'll still need to dispose of them properly. Not doing so, especially if you're somewhere relatively popular for people to travel through, is a problem. You'll need to dispose of the waste appropriately. This is where cleaning the kill site comes in handy. You usually have a few options for this:

1. Take the entrails with you to dispose of at home
2. Bury the entrails,
3. Leave the entrails somewhere other animals can eat it

Taking the entrails home with you can annoy you most times because you have to carry them. This is where extra sealable baggies and trash bags will come in handy, as you can simply zip up the entrails into a bag to carry them, hopefully with no stench or mishaps, and then dispose of them in your trash when you finish your trip.

Burying the entrails is always a popular option, and you can do so simply by digging a deep trench, tossing the entrails in, and putting the dirt back on top. This will allow you to avoid dealing with the entrails as you transport your meat home, and no one will be disturbed by the waste left out. However, you'll need to make sure you don't choose a location near a body of water to bury them. Burying too close to a water source might contaminate it.

Leaving them out for other animals to eat is another option, but you need to be mindful of where you do. You will also need to check if this is even legal where hunting, like many hunting grounds, prohibit this behavior. If it is legal where you are hunting, you can do so safely by moving the entrails somewhere that other people aren't likely to find them and then burying them in a bit of leaf litter somewhere, allowing other animals like mice and foxes to come by and eat their fill. This is perhaps the easiest of the options but isn't available everywhere.

This means that there are also many things that you simply *shouldn't* do when disposing of your entrails. This includes:

1. Dumping them somewhere public.
2. Leaving them out in the open in areas people enjoy, such as hiking trails or in direct eyesight of a hiking trail.
3. Dumping them in or near water.
4. Leaving them on the side of the road.

Keep in mind that the land that you hunt on is likely also enjoyed by other people who want to go about their business without suddenly discovering a pile of half-decayed intestines lying on the side of the path. They want to know that they can enjoy the area as well. By making sure you dispose of your waste appropriately, you ensure that the public opinion of hunters isn't damaged, which could also restrict the ability that you have to hunt further in the future. You want to ensure that hunting is kept sacred. You don't want people to feel a need to petition to restrict hunting, so respect the other people who have a use for the land as well.

SAFE STORAGE

After your meat is cleaned, the next key aspect is getting it down to temperature as quickly as possible. Whether you're going to hang the meat or plan on just taking it home, you want it to be at or below 40 degrees Fahrenheit or 5 degrees celsius to ensure that it doesn't spoil. This can be difficult, depending on where and when you're hunting. Or, it may be easy to simply leave the kill hanging in a game bag from a tree branch if the temperatures are low enough.

If it's not cool enough outdoors for your meat, you'll need to store it in a cooler to reduce the risk of spoilage. However, you might use alternatives to the ice to keep it cool. While ice is cheap and effective, it also melts quickly into a wet mess, and moisture encourages spoilage. Many people will still use ice while making sure their meat is well-stored, such as plastic bags. However, you can also choose to put the meat in other containers, such as game bags. Instead of using ice, you could choose to use frozen water bottles. These will melt much slower, mainly if you use a good cooler.

My favorite cooler is, bar none, the Yeti cooler. However, these are expensive, and that price can be prohibitive for some hunters. A cheaper but still good option is a Coleman steel-belted cooler. They're half the price and will still hold their chill. In a pinch, any cooler that can be sealed that has frozen water bottles in it should do the job. You'll just have to be mindful of how much ice you still have.

Ensuring that you package your meat in the best possible way preserves the meat's natural flavor, color, and taste. Using the wrong containers would mean that the meat would have an altered taste, which could also be unhealthy. To avoid odors and changes in the taste of your meat, it is best to use a healthier packaging option. You can find some of these in regular stores and even on some online hunting stores.

Keep in mind that it's always easier for you to keep your meat clean than clean out the meat later on. So it's so important to be careful. As you prepare your meat, make sure you can drop the temperature of the meat to under 40 F degrees/ 5 C degrees, but prevent it from freezing. Remember that this temperature doesn't kill bacteria—it slows the growth, so it is still susceptible to spoilage if you're not careful.

Before you store your meat, remember that you should rinse off as much of the blood as possible and scrape away any blood that has already coagulated. The pH of blood makes it particularly susceptible to growing bacteria. Get rid of the water used before putting the meat into a game bag to protect it. Remember, game bags are preferred over plastic in most cases because they're breathable, and this allows the meat to chill quicker.

If the air is not cool enough for you to leave your meat out, get a cooler with some ice packs that won't melt into water. This will allow you to chill the meat without worrying about excess moisture. Some coolers can keep their chill for several days sometimes. Choosing a safe storage option is the perfect way to keep your meat fresh for longer.

(Tip: One trick that I love to use is adding citric acid. This mild organic acid can be sprayed right onto your meat to help keep your meat safer. It will slow down the growth of bacteria, which can make the difference between good or lousy meat if you're traveling with it in warm weather.)

☰ TRANSPORTATION

Finally, it's essential to consider how to transport your meat home. One consideration is how you get home—did you drive there? Did you fly somewhere on a hunting trip? Did you travel for several days to get there? Depending upon how far away you are, you'll have different options to bring your harvest home. If you live relatively close to the hunting grounds, simply bagging it up and driving home with the meat in a cooler should be enough. However, if you've got a long trip ahead of you, you'll need to make sure whatever you're using to carry your meat will be durable enough to keep the meat cool, clean, and safe while still fitting any restrictions you may have.

The simplest way to do this is to start by putting everything in sealable bags or containers. Ziploc bags or something similar work well because they will be easily stored flat when they're not in use, and you'll be able to pack them tightly into a cooler if necessary. When using zipper bags of any kind that seal, using ice will be suitable.

Store your meat in a durable cooler for hunting. If you took a styrofoam cooler out into the field with you because it was lighter, it probably wouldn't be durable enough for you to travel with. This is especially the case if you fly home from your hunting trip. When you fly home, you want to be sure that your cooler won't leak. If you're flying, use the cooler as a carry-on and check it between flights to make sure you don't need to replace the ice.

When you get home, make sure it gets moved straight into a fridge or freezer, depending upon how you want to store the meat. Keep in mind that it may last just 3-5 days before it needs to get used or frozen when you store your meat. When frozen, it can last another 1-2 years, depending upon how you've taken to freezing it. (Tip: Freezing in vacuum-sealed packages will keep it the freshest for the longest.)

3

THE ESSENTIAL GUIDE TO SMALL GAME

Before you get out there and get active, you must understand the ins and outs of the animals you may be encountering. Whether you choose to hunt, knowing more about that animal, what they're likely to do, and how you can leave with a successful bounty will help you immensely. As you read through this chapter, you're getting an essential guide to several common animals.

The first bit of information you're going to get is the habitat for each animal. We'll go over where you're likely to find these animals, as well as when they're likely to be more active. It's easier to hunt certain animals at specific times of the year. By knowing where to look for animals, you dramatically boost your chance of success.

Next, you'll be introduced to key techniques that will help you track the game you're trying to find. By knowing how to track the animals that you'd like to hunt, you'll be more likely to find them as well.

Third, you'll receive some key tips to hunt each of the listed animals successfully. These tips should help you boost your chances of getting your hands on something good. Just being able to spot an animal isn't the only thing that counts—you also have to catch and kill it in a way that doesn't render the meat inedible, and that also isn't inhumane. You've got to balance honoring the life of the kill with being able to keep the meat edible. Some of these animals, such as snapping turtles and bullfrogs, are incredibly difficult to kill, while other animals are so small that it's challenging to shoot them without ruining the flesh. Hopefully, armed with the correct weapon and all the information that you'll need, you'll find that this process is made significantly easier.

≡ A FIELD GUIDE TO SQUIRRELS

When it's time to hunt squirrels, there are four types that you're likely to find, depending on where you live. These are fox squirrels, gray squirrels, Abert's squirrels, and pine squirrels. They each look distinctive in their ways.

Fox squirrels are larger than other species. Their fur is mostly grey, but they've got a rusty orange color to their tails and underbellies. They live in smaller woods that have open areas. They're most commonly found in the eastern part of the United States.

Gray squirrels are the most common ones throughout the region, and eastern gray squirrels are commonly actually black, brown, grey, or white, while western grays are found along the west coast.

Abert's squirrels have long grey-black tufts on their ears and darker fur with white underbellies. They don't store food instead of eating pine needles, cones, and bark during the winter. They can be found in western and southwestern portions of the United States.

Pine squirrels are found on the west coast and are small reddish squirrels. These are the most vocal, so if they catch you hunting, they're likely to warn all the other squirrels in the area as well.

HABITAT

Squirrels are found predominantly in trees, which they use both as a source of shelter and to get their food. Squirrels mostly eat nuts, with the preferred nuts varying from location to location. These intelligent animals know that hiding in the trees is one of the best ways they can avoid being eaten by predators, and they'll do what they can to avoid being out in the open if they sense that danger is near. This means that when you want to hunt them, you're going to have a hard time finding them.

The trees make for the perfect shelter for them since most predators can't get through the branches. Foxes, coyotes, and other animals on the ground can't get them as soon as they climb into a tree. While some felines can get at them in the trees, they can run to the tips of the branches they're on, which won't support the weight of most of them. And, when hawks or falcons go after them, they can dart through the branches much better than the birds can navigate through them while flying.

Of course, this means that you're going to be hard-pressed to get a squirrel as soon as it gets into the branches. If you want to track and kill your squirrel successfully, you'll need to draw them out into the open without them detecting your presence.

TRACKING

Tracking a squirrel isn't as hard as you might think, but it requires a *lot* of patience. Be willing to sit around and wait for something to appear. If you know that squirrels present from other signs, such as seeing chewed-up branches, the husks of nuts, or you can hear them nearby, you know that you're in the right spot. From there, it's all about waiting it out until one wanders in your path.

No squirrel will wander in front of you if you're out making a racket around you. Be quiet about it if you want to coax them to feel comfortable enough to appear in your area. To look for signs of a squirrel, consider these points:

- **Squirrel nests:** These look like balls of leaves with a few twigs poking out. They enter inside from the side, along the branch. If you can spot these nests, there's a good chance of squirrels in the general area.
- **Shredded nuts on the ground:** After a squirrel digs up acorns, they prefer to eat them right there. They'll tear the acorn shells up into smaller pieces, which you'll find all over the ground.
- **Bark biting:** Squirrels will chew along the most common routes they take as they go up and down trees. This leaves a scent mark on them, especially as they rub their cheeks over them. These will look like long, chewed-up strips of bark.

TIPS FOR SUCCESSFUL HUNTING

When you choose to hunt squirrels, the first thing to keep in mind is that they are rarely active when the weather is terrible. Squirrels are the most active in the first hours of daybreak and the later afternoon. This means that the best time to head out would be the first hours of the morning, especially if it's sunny. They avoid being out in bad weather, just like you probably want to do as well. If you're going to have better luck catching squirrels, consider these tips.

Still hunting

When you still hunt, you sit quietly and wait for the squirrels to come to your area. Hiding somewhere that serves as a natural hiding spot should encourage squirrels to slowly move around more than they feel comfortable that there are no threats around. These animals will often alert their friends in the trees, so you want to be out of sight as much as possible.

Once you've identified a squirrel, you can slowly and carefully stalk them from tree to tree. This involves carefully moving from one area to the next, moving slowly and quietly while listening and scanning the area. You also must make sure the background is safe to shoot before getting ready to do so.

Throw Rocks

Sometimes, you can fool squirrels into thinking that there's another predator somewhere else if you throw rocks against trees. This may make a squirrel appear as it bolts from one area to find somewhere else safe. However, they don't give you a very long window of opportunity before they're off. You'll need to be ready to make a quick shot.

Squirrel calls

You can mimic the sounds squirrels make with a few common tactics. You could always buy a squirrel call that will do it for you, or you can use your gun and some coins. A coin against the butt plate may imitate the barking sound squirrels make, while two coins together can mimic feeding chatter. This could entice some reluctant squirrels to make their presence known.

Leaf Sounds

When squirrels sense predators, they remain still and out of sight. If you want to encourage a squirrel to approach, one of the easiest ways to do so is to make it sound like squirrels are active in the area again. By stirring at leaves around you, making quick rustling sounds in the leaves in a broken pattern, you mimic the sound of a digging squirrel looking for food. This should mean that it is safe for other squirrels to approach.

Hunt with a Partner

Squirrels are brilliant. They are well-known for running a circle around a tree, constantly staying out of your sights by keeping the tree between you and them. However, if you have a second person there to hunt with you, you can have one person sitting out of sight while the other person makes the squirrel move. The hunter can then shoot.

A FIELD GUIDE TO RABBITS

Rabbits are quick. However, their meat is almost unparalleled in taste. If you want to hunt rabbits, you'll need to know where to spot them. Thankfully, they're relatively easy to find because they prefer places where they can take care of all their needs in one go. They want to know that they can get food, water, and shelter within a relatively small area.

HABITAT

Typically, rabbits will eat as close to their cover as possible, nibbling on grass, shoots, or flowers. They'll also happily enjoy grain from fields or bark from trees. They rarely require too much water, so waiting next to a water source isn't the most effective answer. They're able to keep water from their foods easily, so they'll avoid water if they think it's dangerous.

Typically, you want to hunt in areas with thick cover if you want a rabbit. They'll hide in briars or in areas where the native grass grows thick. The grass provides a source of food and a place where they can hide. They will hide underground as well, taking up unused burrows from digging animals. They'll live their entire lives in a relatively small range of space, usually a few acres at a time, so you'll need to keep this in mind before hunting. If you can find signs of a rabbit nearby, you know it's somewhere close.

TRACKING

Being able to track rabbits will help you immensely when hunting. From being able to spot their footprints to signs of scat or that they've been eating lately, you will do much better on your hunt if you can spot where they are.

Signs of scat

Rabbit scat is a simple way to find out whether there are rabbits nearby as well. They are tiny pellets, between ¼ to ½ inch in diameter. It's round and somewhat wrinkly or fibrous. If there is snow on the ground, it may also be marked with orange or reddish urine. They usually leave behind just a few pellets at a time unless they've been there for a while.

Signs of rabbit snacks

When you identify rabbit scat in a pile, you'll also probably find signs of feeding. Typically, the signs of feeding are little snippets in the stems and wood. You'll notice a clean 45-degree cut when twigs are less than ½ inch in diameter.

Bark gnawing

Rabbits will gnaw at wood if they don't have any other opportunity to get the food they need. If you notice the other signs and nibbles on bark near levels that the rabbits can reach, there's probably a rabbit nearby.

TIPS FOR SUCCESSFUL HUNTING

To hunt successfully, you'll need first to track down signs that there are rabbits nearby. Then, be able to get started. To make it easier, consider these different actions as well.

Rabbit dogs

Rabbit dogs are incredibly beneficial. Those who know how to hunt and are trained well can lead the rabbit right back to where you're ready to hunt it. However, you will need to make sure that the dog is trained for the task. Even then, your dog may go after the rabbit as soon as you shoot it, ruining it to retrieve the flesh.

Walk or stalk

When you hunt on your own, you may need to walk through the cover to make the rabbit run or stalk it somewhere near a rabbit's habitat. Walking works well in a group, primarily if you can communicate when you've flushed a rabbit out, and it's heading toward someone else. Stalking is best alone, especially in the winter, where you can track steps. Keep in mind that by the time you spot a rabbit, it's probably already been watching you. You'll need to be careful not to spook it.

Hunt along edges

Natural edges take advantage of rabbits' habitat, such as the line between a forest and a field or heavy cover and somewhere less populated. Hunting along the edges means you're more likely to spot a rabbit.

A FIELD GUIDE TO GROUSE AND PARTRIDGES

HABITAT

Grouse and partridges eat both plants and insects, with acorns being a staple in the winter months to increase body fat for spring reproduction. They may enjoy berries, shoots, and other nuts as well when they can find them. They are not very picky! While they require water like all other animals, they can usually get enough food or drink from morning dew. They only seek standing or running water out readily when it's been dry, or they'll also enjoy it if they stumble upon it along with their foraging.

Typically, it's more important for you to consider the shelter of the grouse/partridge when trying to find them. They love to live in wooded areas—in particular, they love forests. They rarely hide in the trees unless they're threatened, but they enjoy the woody cover.

They will usually stay within a mile of where they were hatched, meaning that it's relatively easy to find them. The male's drum in the spring attracts females and has even smaller ranges than females, who will follow the drumming male and hunt down their nesting site.

For the best of luck, go hunting on sunny days in the fall, when there's just a little wind. You may hear them walking around during this time. They're most active late and early in the day, but you may find them. However, when it's windy, they'll stay hidden in trees.

TRACKING

If you're interested in finding grouse/partridge, one of the best ways to do so is to locate areas where there are acorns all over the ground. This is especially the case in the fall if you want to find birds enjoying them.

As you walk around, consider pausing if you think that a grouse/partridge might be present. They sit still as long as you're walking by them at a steady pace. However, if you stop moving, they may think they've been found, and instead of remaining in place, they'll run. This means that you'll have the opportunity to get them.

(Tip: The easiest way to track them is to walk or drive down gravel dirt roads. The grouse/partridge eats little rocks for their digestive system. They tend to stand still if they are spooked, so catching them off guard on the road gives you a wide-open shot.)

TIPS FOR SUCCESSFUL HUNTING

Grouse/Partridge hunting isn't always easy. You're looking for a small bird that can easily hide or fly away, and you're in it's habitat. It can be even harder to locate your kill after shooting one, especially if you have no clue where it may have gone. Consider these important tips if you want to hunt grouse/partridge effectively.

Start scouting the area in spring

Since these birds don't stray far from where they hatched, you'll know where they'll be in fall by looking in the spring for the birds. You'll be able to listen for the drumming males in the spring to get a general idea of where they're likely to populate. You may even hear chicks chirping to tell you where they have been nesting. By finding these locations, you'll be likely to find grouse ready for hunting in the fall as well.

Finding Prime Habitat

Grouse/Partridge prefers to nest in areas where a forest has begun a secondary succession. This means that the area has had some significant disturbance, such as a fire or natural storm that decimated the original plants. Then, 5 to 12 years after that point, there is new growth thriving in the secondary succession. This is prime land for grouse, and you're likely to find them.

Second Flushes

When a bird flies uphill to avoid you, it won't go as far as a bird that is flying downhill. Usually, it's easier to hunt those going uphill than those going downhill.

A FIELD GUIDE TO DOVES

Doves, especially mourning doves, are a tasty choice if you want to hunt them. Most hunters are likely to focus on where they feed, and for a good reason. If you're going to find your doves to catch, the best thing you can do is know where you should be looking. These birds can pose a bit of a challenge as they move quickly through the air. However, if you know what you're doing, they can be caught.

HABITAT

Doves eat seeds primarily, which means that looking in areas where weeds and grass grow and produce seeds is a great way to hunt them down. They have feet designed for perching, so you'll want to look for areas where they can perch to get their food.

They'll also go out of the way to get water at least twice per day. This is easy during wet seasons, but they're likely to visit ponds and streams during dryer seasons. In particular, they need somewhere they can get water, and if you find areas where they can get water without cover, you may catch them drinking. Doves migrate, flying north in the summer and south in the fall and winter, so plan your season accordingly.

TRACKING

Before you get started with hunting, you'll need to know how to track them. Typically, the best thing you can do is choose a location to hunt and stick to it. If you've chosen a suitable location, the birds should come. Keep these tips in mind to ensure you're tracking well.

Scouting layouts

Scouting the layout is about spending a few days viewing the field before you decide to hunt it. You want to know what you're working with. You want to know what's going on with the area before you choose to hunt there. Get to know what a day or two of activity looks like before jumping into the action. Sometimes, seeing what happens at dawn will show you what you can expect to see the next day. Watch the birds early on to notice their habits. You'll also get the ability to understand the flight paths they take. The flight paths that they take are usually the paths they leave as well.

High ground

Look for the high ground before you get started. The high spots are the most likely to attract doves. It becomes a natural flight target. If you can stand between a hill and somewhere woody, you've got an excellent chance to see some doves flying over.

Near water

Setting up by the water in the afternoon is a great way to catch doves who need to get some drinks before heading off to roost for the night. They want places that are low with little brush so they can land and see their surroundings.

TIPS FOR SUCCESSFUL HUNTING

To up your chances of catching doves, there are a few steps that will help you.

Shoot high birds

Shooting high means shooting overhead birds and within your range. However, this is also one of the most challenging shots to make if you don't know what you're doing.

Use a retriever

Because hunting should not produce waste, it might be easier to have a retriever to help if you're hunting in a heavily planted field. A good retriever will be able to help you find birds quicker and easier.

Look for activity

Every so often throughout the afternoon, there will be periods where the doves fly about more often. They will fly for 5 or 10 minutes, then be relatively inactive. Keeping track of this and being ready to land your shots will help.

Follow through with the swing

When you shoot doves, one of the most common mistakes is cutting the swing of the shot short. As you track your target, you're swinging to keep your gun aiming at it. If you don't continue the swing after pulling the trigger, you're going to miss the shot.

☰ A FIELD GUIDE TO QUAILS AND PHEASANTS

Hunting quail/Pheasants can be highly exciting as you make your way through hunting. These birds depend highly on the weather because they can't store enough energy for extended cold periods. This means that they must go out into the snow to hunt as much as they can. This is especially important to consider because they can't dig easily through the snow. When you can find them, however, you get a huge benefit: They taste amazing.

HABITAT

Quail/Pheasants are edge species—they prefer to live in areas with dense covers within walking distance for food. They primarily enjoy waste grain in fields or weed seeds. If you can find somewhere with these criteria, you're likely to find quail/pheasant around as well. The best area to find them is within about 25 yards of the edge between a weedy field and a cultivated grain field.

Typically, they get enough water from morning dew and rarely seek out watering holes unless it's been exceptionally dry lately. They're left too vulnerable to water holes and try to avoid being out in the open.

Once you locate a covey of quails/pheasants, you're likely to continue to find them in the same area each year. They'll come to the exact location if they consistently get the resources they need to survive.

TRACKING

When you want to track quail/pheasant, there are a few places you can look that are usually likely to provide what you're looking for. However, lately, there has been a decline in wild quail/pheasant as they lose their habitat, so you may find it harder to locate them. Typically, they are found somewhere that is both open and woody. They like briars and other areas that will keep them covered.

Keep in mind the following:

- Quail/Pheasants like to enjoy seeds in the fields in the morning.
- They like to rest midday under some cover.
- They like a snack in the afternoon on the weedy field.
- They sleep in grassy, weedy areas at night.

TIPS FOR SUCCESSFUL HUNTING

The hunting process for quail and pheasants can be tedious as you go through looking for them. However, you can make it easier for yourself by remembering and implementing tips such as the following:

Get a hunting dog

A good hunting dog is highly effective for flushing out quail. Make sure that your dog is well-trained, so they don't rush and scare birds. Training a dog to use a slow approach to get close will help to flush them out.

Practice Marksmanship

One of the most critical skills you'll need is to train yourself to shoot to kill. Quail and pheasants are quick and skilled at flying. If you can't shoot quickly in a wave of confusion, you're going to miss the kill. To help with this, try practicing shooting with a friend, having them throw several targets in a quick rush while you try to shoot them down.

Know the Habits

Quail and pheasants are very predictable. They'll repeatedly come to the same fields, will rest, and eat at the same time. By learning the routines of the quail you're hunting, be able to eliminate a lot of the confusion of where they are at any point in time.

Look for the Covey Rise

When you flush out a covey of quail/pheasant, and they all rush up, you may feel quite excited about it. You're probably going to be thrilled to see them all at once. However, keep in mind that you should focus on one bird at a time. Usually, you can take one or two at a time within a few seconds as you get better at hunting.

A FIELD GUIDE TO DUCKS

Hunting ducks is a bit of a difficult pastime if you don't know what you're doing, but it can be deliciously fulfilling. Traditionally, hunters hide in a blind either over water or in a field, while hunters display decoys to make it look like other ducks are already there.

The purpose of this is to lure other birds to the area. If they see other ducks and geese hanging out in the area, they will assume it's a safe place to rest and enjoy some food, so they'll take some time to land there as well.

The best way to know how to get started with ducks is to make sure that you scout areas before. Make sure you choose locations that birds have already traditionally visited to ensure that you make it convincing.

HABITAT

As waterfowl, ducks will be found near water. They need this for roosting and loafing. They will need to return to the water at some point, so if you can find the water, you're likely also to find them. If you've seen them hiding in these areas on their own already, you're likely to hunt them in the coming days.

Look for areas with shallow wetlands filled with seed-producing plants, especially in the early season. They'll enjoy being able to munch on the plants that they can find. Rivers, marshes, creeks, open water, or even flooded fields, such as rice or soybeans, are quick to attract ducks because of the water and food. Make sure that you check the policies for hunting, and you check whether you can legally hunt in the area where you're scoping out ducks. You may try to hunt on developed land.

Typically, most people will come in to hunt on an opening day for the season. You're likely to find that you've got plenty of newly hatched birds making their first migration, and they'll be much easier to trick than others who have had a few rodeos and know what to look out for.

You want to pay attention to the weather when hunting as well. When there's a strong north wind, or when the weather is colder, you'll find that birds are flying south, looking for warmth. If you're hunting, sunshine and wind will be perfect. This is especially the case for mallards, who may also choose to stick it out as the weather cools.

Sometimes, you may even find that ducks will return north during the season. When there is a freeze that pushes them south, followed by a quick thaw, they will often return to the area they just left, at which point they're less wary than they were before as well. You may also find that at the very end of the season, as birds move north to their breeding grounds, you might catch some. They are so caught up trying to get back for a mating that they forget to pay attention to prevent themselves from being hunted.

TRACKING

You ultimately have five different options for hunting and tracking ducks. If you're somewhere where ducks remain, you're likely to find them in the water. You can choose to hunt them through these options:

1. Decoys: With this method, you set out decoys all over a field or in the water and then hide in a blind to wait for the birds to come around. Then, when they land, you can hunt.
2. Pass shooting: This involves shooting at flight lines as they pass in your shotgun range. You essentially figure out how the birds are flying, stay in the line, and wait for them to come by. You then shoot as they pass over you.
3. Jump shooting: With jump shooting, you sneak up on ducks on the water, then fire as they take flight. This is typically done near shorelines.
4. Float hunts: This involves floating on a river in either a canoe or a kayak and shooting at unsuspecting birds. You'll have to depend on the river during this time, which can be difficult as well.
5. Skull boat shoots: This form of hunting involves using a skiff and paddle to get within the shooting range of ducks. Then, you'll have to shoot quickly. This is perhaps the hardest of the methods.

TIPS FOR SUCCESSFUL HUNTING

If you want to hunt ducks, you need to keep in mind that they can be a bit difficult. Most birds can be tricky to hunt, but this is especially the case with smaller ones. This means that you need to be prepared with a vast arsenal to help you with the process.

Don't forget the camo

Camo is essential to keeping yourself hidden. However, if you're going to be hunting on a kayak or some other boat, you want to keep your boat concealed as well. You can do this with a camo cord. Essentially, you just put some cord across your kayak that's been spaced roughly a foot apart and then weave in a bunch of natural vegetation found in the area. This will help you conceal the boat from sight and may even remain in place all season long if you're careful. You'll have an easier time sneaking up on everything in this manner.

Hunt later

Typically, ducks will migrate with cold fronts so they can use the strong tailwinds. If you have a cold front coming through your area, make sure you don't leave early. Stay later into the morning so you can be there when flocks may stop to take a rest before getting on their way.

Know when to remove the decoys

While decoys can be a great tool for you, they can also put you at a serious disadvantage if you don't know what you're doing. Many ducks may be afraid of them, especially later in the season when they realize that all the stationary ducks they've seen seem to show that there will be shots fired. If the decoys remain in place, they're likely to have problems. Late in the season, pull them in and use calls instead.

Be patient

This should be a rule for all the games you're hunting. Patience is a virtue. It's a huge mistake if you accidentally flush out all the ducks from the roost before dawn has even hit. If you wait for first light and the ducks to spread out on their own before creeping out to set up shop, you're less likely to startle away the ducks, and you'll likely have the ducks return later on to rest, meaning that overall, you'll have more shooting opportunities.

Check the winds

Pay attention to the wind so you can position the decoys and blinds. If you can't tell which way the wind is blowing, you can try squeezing a bit of talcum powder or fine soil in the air and see which way it goes. That's the direction the wind is blowing.

Camouflage the gun

While you might hide with white gloves and jackets, you still need to hide your shotgun. These are highly visible in the snow, especially if you're also wearing all white. You want to consider covering up your barrel with white medical gauze to hide it while hunting in snowy conditions.

A FIELD GUIDE TO TURKEYS

Turkeys eat a wide range of things out in the wild, starting on bugs and quickly moving to acorns and fresh greens. The fatty nuts they eat prepare them to survive for the winter while also providing them with a delicious taste. They can usually be spotted in the early morning, hunting for grasshoppers or sipping at the water. If you want to track them down, you'll need first to know where to look.

HABITAT

Typically, you'll find turkeys hunting for food or water. On spring days, they may not need to visit water sources if it's rained recently - they can enjoy standing in water puddles or on leaves. Tracking water sources is a great way to spot where these birds are at any point in time.

Turkeys will usually stick to a relatively small range—typically only 2000 acres. Toms will spend their time in even more limited ranges because the females come to the males while the females roam. The entire flock is likely to stick to the same range unless disturbed, and when they leave, there's a good chance that more birds will enter the area.

TRACKING

The best thing that you can do when tracking turkeys is to start with scouting. Start by looking for signs of dropped feathers, scratches, and strut marks on the grounds, or even droppings. Tracks are commonly found as well, especially near water sources.

It's usually a good idea to scout the week before you're ready to hunt. This will help you spot out the various areas where the turkeys prefer to stay. You should also make it a point to track early in the morning. If you get lucky, you'll find a male strutting and attracting females. As he courts his hens, he's more or less setting up his own space. He's going to stay in that area unless you disturb him. If you wait for him in the morning, you're likely to find him around in the afternoon in a similar area. Setting up where he was in the morning is the best way to find him in the afternoon. And, if you watch his routine over a few days, you're more likely to find them. They will stick to the same routine as much as they can, making them easy to predict.

TIPS FOR SUCCESSFUL HUNTING

When you're out hunting, there are several things that you can do to help boost your chances of success. Remember these tips if you want to have a good chance at catching your turkey. Turkeys have a grand vision, so they're likely to see you if you're moving too much.

Camouflage matters

The best thing that you can do when you're hunting turkey ensures that you can camouflage yourself. Make sure that you're hiding somewhere that they can't see you, and use camouflage on your tools. Turkeys will know what to look out for—they'll see your skin or hair as a sign to run. They may even notice a flash of teeth. Their vision is exceptional, and you need to hide well.

Stillness

Just camouflage isn't enough either. You need to remain as still as possible. They're likely to catch you if you're moving around too much as the camouflage will move with it. They've got great vision, and if you're not careful to be still and silent, the turkey is likely to leave quickly before you spot it.

Use a blind or large tree

A blind can be your best tool when hunting turkeys. If you can't use a blind, you'll need a tree that's big enough that your silhouette will be hidden, and you'll be able to sit in the shadows as much as possible. However, in a blind, you'll be able to move around a bit more, and you'll be able to enjoy coffee or something else inside of it, as turkeys can't smell.

Don't stalk it

Stalking turkeys is rarely a good idea. Turkeys are much more likely to spot your movements if you're trying to stalk them when they're out of range and you try to approach them. Instead, you can remember what they're doing and where they're doing it so you can focus on them in the future. You're likely to find them better if you do.

A FIELD GUIDE TO GEESE

Canada geese are well known for their wide range of migrations. They fly south in wide V formations that are quick to catch the eye of all who see them. However, for hunters, this marks the beginning of a very important time: Hunting season.

Canada goose hunting has become very specialized lately, with people creating calling tools and more just to get the kill. They have learned the ins and outs of being able to lure geese in to use for their own, and you can learn some serious tips to do the same as well.

HABITAT

Geese will be found in primarily the same habitat as ducks and other waterfowl. You can expect them to be enjoying time in wet places, from rivers to lakes and more. They don't care where the water source is, and they just want to have somewhere they can hide and meet their needs.

Geese will display where they're at, however, announcing their presence with their cries. They will usually travel in large flocks, in huge V-shaped wedges. They'll break up here and there, but if you call the geese as you see and hear them, you may attract them to you.

They travel south for the winter and then north again in the warmer summers, riding on the tails of cold fronts, so pay close attention to the weather. They're a bit more likely to hunker down in cold weather than ducks are, and they aren't about digging out their holes in the snow to eat.

TRACKING

Rather than tracking geese, it's more about waiting for them to arrive. Like with ducks, one of the best ways to lure them in is to set up a blind so they can't locate you and then set up decoys, remembering that as the season goes on, they're likely to be hesitant to approach them if they don't know the source. You'll likely want to study their habits before hunting, and remember that you are better off waiting to settle in after they've already taken off for their morning feeding.

You might enjoy setting up an elaborate blind, but keep in mind that after a few shots, you're likely to spook the birds to move elsewhere, at which point, you can either find another body of water, or you can wait for more to fly in.

Remember that while tracking these birds, you must be as motionless as possible and only shoot when they've approached you enough that you know you can catch them. Keep in mind that if you notice they seem wary, they're probably spotting something that makes them nervous. You might need to change up your layout if you want to attract them to your area. They may look reluctant about landing, or they might even take off at the last minute instead of landing within your range. These geese are growing increasingly wary, which means it will be challenging to catch them.

TIPS FOR SUCCESSFUL HUNTING

To hunt geese successfully, several tips can help you immensely with the process. Knowing how to call to set up your decoys, you're likely to attract geese your way. Figure out what works best for you and change your strategy if something isn't working for you any longer.

The Call

Goose calls can be beneficial to entice birds to land within your range. You can get them in three different styles: Resonant chambers, flutes, and short-reeds. Typically, resonant chambers are the easiest to use, but they're also very limited. You can't make as many sounds. Flute calls are harder to use but make more sounds, but they're also usually mellower. Short-reed calls will have the widest range of sounds and are louder, with less air needed than the other options. The short-reed call is the favored variety among hunters and will be your best bet if you're serious about hunting geese.

Setting up Decoys

Decoys will be vital, and you'll want to set them up in areas with brilliant cover for you. Your job is to remain covered, and if you can hunt where you can hide, you're going to see significant improvements in your ability to hunt. Find rows of grass that might have a dip in terrain where you'd be able to hide as well. Avoid getting yourself stuck in the same place for too long, however, or the geese will get to know where you are.

Don't choose several different decoys

If you're not wise with the decoys you set up, then you can run into trouble. This is especially true if you mix them up and create a mismatched look that sets the geese off that there's something wrong. Stick to just one kind of decoy for the best results.

Stay out of the way

While it might be convenient to place yourself in line with the bird's approach, you're also going to scare them off when they recognize the signs that hunters are present. Instead of being where the geese are, place yourself ten yards to the side of where they'll be landing or parallel with the wind. This will help you stay hidden, and you're more likely to land the shot.

A FIELD GUIDE TO BULLFROGS

North American bullfrogs are the largest frogs that you can locate in North America, and vary from greens to browns, and are usually somewhat blotchy. They also taste great when you fry frog legs. These frogs have been appearing and spreading throughout North America, out-competing other native frog species, and are invasive in many areas. They're quite large and are starving, so they'll continue to seek out new waters and expand their range, little by little. They were initially introduced in the early 1900s as a food source and expanded their territory.

Hunting these animals can be tricky, as they're tough to kill effectively, but hunting them can yield plenty of food for you to enjoy. Their meat tastes like a cross between fish and chicken and can be an enjoyable addition to your diet. There's a good chance that you're likely to find them with a bit of perseverance, and you can catch them with a net, a fishing rod, or even your hands if you wanted to.

They're willing to eat just about anything they can get their tongues on, including fish, mice, or even snakes. They're not afraid of much, but they will run away from you if you try to catch them.

Keep in mind that you need to know what the laws are for hunting bullfrogs in your area. Some places may require you to kill them before you transport them.

HABITAT

Bullfrogs will live anywhere they can find food. They're invasive on the western side of the continent, and they're easy to find just about anywhere you'd find other frogs. Look for them in ponds and lakes, and you're bound to find them lurking beneath the water's surface.

Many people hunt for them at night, choosing to shine flashlights and look for the reflections of their eyes.

To find them, look in ponds and marshes. Listen in the evening before going out to hunt—you'll hear their calls and will know that you're in the right spot. They'll usually all croak together. It's a loud, deep croak.

TRACKING

Tracking bullfrogs is as simple as listening for their tell-tale cry. You'll hear the tell-tale guttural noises they make, and you're also likely to see them around. If you're hunting at night, you'll be able to see the reflections of their eyes in the water. However, if you're somewhere where frogs can be heard, and you're in bullfrog territory, there are probably bullfrogs present as well.

TIPS FOR SUCCESSFUL HUNTING

Hunting bullfrogs can be tricky if you don't know what you're doing, especially if you go into it bare-handed. They are quick to spook, and they'll often dart right out of your reach if you're not careful. However, if you're armed with a fishing pole, you're likely to catch them. By using a hook just right, you can fish them up quickly. Alternatively, you can chase them down and use your hands, a bucket, a net, or anything else. Even pronged grabbers you can use to snap them up to pull them in if you wanted to. You could even shoot one if you had a gun and were close enough, but this isn't the most recommended way to do so.

Hooking a bobber

One of the more efficient ways to catch a bullfrog is to put a hook directly on top and on the bottom of a bobber, with some sort of lure to catch them. You can add a bit of bait or grasshopper onto one end of the hook. Then, wait for the frog to latch onto it and reel them in.

Hunt at nighttime

It's easier to see bullfrogs at night. They're more likely to come out on land when it's no longer sunny enough to dry them out almost immediately after they go out. To monitor them, you can use an LED flashlight to search for them slowly. Bigger bullfrogs will have wide-set eyes that are further apart than most other eyes you see.

Use a canoe if possible

Your footprints are likely to startle away any bullfrogs you're hunting down, even if you try your hardest to be quiet as you go. It's better to make it a point to slowly creep up on a canoe in the water, moving gently than to walk along the shore. But, if you are hunting on land, just try to move as quietly as you can.

Jacking bullfrogs

By shining a bright light into the bullfrog within about 10 yards, you can "jack" the bullfrog. You essentially put the frog in a trance, similar to how deer pause at headlights. This allows you to rush toward it and catch it with your bare hands or with anything else that you have.

Remember to be firm, but not too firm

Don't grab a bullfrog too roughly. We're not out trying to hurt them, and just because we're hunting them doesn't mean that we need to forget about their comfort and well-being. Don't cause unnecessary pain by squeezing them. Hold them with the same pressure you'd use on a bar of soap, and hold them grasping around upper thighs and legs held together so they can't jump away.

Kill it quickly

If you're trying to kill the bullfrog, you can either bash their head or cut off their head. They are known for making you think they're dead, only to try to rush away mid-skinning suddenly. You want to desensitize it and then kill it. A few swift blows to the head should do it. Make sure it's fully dead before you skin it. Some people prefer removing the head before field dressing to make sure the frog is dead.

A FIELD GUIDE TO SNAPPING TURTLES

If you live somewhere filled with snapping turtles, the first thing that you need to do is confirm that you may hunt them where you live or where you are going. You may choose to use traps, or you might simply snatch one up if the opportunity arises. Either way, hunting for a turtle can provide you with a delicious meal. One of the easiest ways to get your hands on a snapping turtle is to create a trap for them and set it out somewhere that will help you catch it.

Keep in mind that snapping turtles are dangerous: If you put your hand in harm's way, they can bite your finger right off. They're also quick and can flip themselves over, so even if you think that you've flipped one over and it'll be okay to grab, think again. Their claws are also quite dangerous. However, when you grab them by their tails and hold them out of reach of your body, they can't do anything at all.

Spotting a snapping turtle as opposed to other turtles that may be less dangerous is pretty straightforward. They usually have duller shells that may even be covered in moss or algae. Its tail and head won't retract fully either. And you'll notice that they have sharp claws on yellow feet, plus a massive, thick neck. They can also move quickly on land.

HABITAT

Snapping turtles can be found in a wide range of North America, from Southern Alberta to Central Texas in the US. They live only in either fresh or brackish water but prefer water muddy and loaded with plant life. This allows them to hide easier, meaning they can snag their prey easier than well. They will usually spend their time in the water but will make their way onto land when it's time to lay eggs.

They can be found in many types of water and aren't that picky, so long as it isn't saltwater. They can be found in lakes, ponds, streams, rivers, or even marshes and swamps. They're solitary creatures that rarely have many social interactions beyond mating.

Keep in mind that they may even bury themselves in mud, leaving only their eyes and nostrils exposed. They may even leave out their tongues, which they wiggle around in the water to attract fish to eat.

TRACKING

Typically, you don't track turtles. You either find them or you don't. It's usually to set up a snapping turtle trap, which you can use to help yourself find them. Follow these steps for a simple turtle trap that will help you catch some in no time.

1. Start with a long strip of chicken wire. It should be large enough to create a wire trap roughly 2 feet in diameter. Then, using tie wire, tie each of the holes as you work your way up, essentially stitching the chicken wire. Do so up four feet.

2. Cut the wire above the last two feet. You'll have a strip of wire that's 6 feet x 2 feet.

3. Take the flat piece of wire to the top of your 4' tube, attach it all the way around with tie wire, and then cut off the excess. This closes off the trap. Put the closed end down with the open end facing up.

4. Take a dip net and cut off 7-8 inches, having an open end on each side.

5. Put the narrow end of the dip net inside the cage. Then, tie the rest of it to the top of the trap. Use strong nylon to do this, weaving it in place.

6. Cut a doorway using a wire cutter to create 10 inches on two sides of the door and 16 inches on the last side. This can be opened and closed to let you reach into the trap.

7. Use a foot of nylon string to tie to the narrow end of the dip net on each side of the trap to create a funnel.

8. Tie some bait a foot away from the narrow end of the dip net and make sure the turtle can't get it without entering the trap.

TIPS FOR SUCCESSFUL HUNTING

Set the trap somewhere it's not going to drown the turtle

When you are hunting, you don't want to drown the turtle before you get out unintentionally. You'll like the trap to be designed so the turtle can't somehow dislodge it and make it fall into the water. If the turtle drowns, it probably won't still be fresh by the time you get it.

Choose good bait

The bait wins over snapping turtles. Make it a point to choose out bait like chicken or fish that it can smell, but it won't reach unless it gets into the trap. This should help you ensure you get your catch.

Stun before killing

Snapping turtles are dangerous. You're going to want to stun it before you reach inside of it. The best way to do this is to smash it in the head, pushing it inward toward the shell.

4

STEP-BY-STEP HOW TO FIELD DRESS

Man has traditionally had to turn to hunt; it has been part of the human heritage since the beginning of time. If you don't hunt, you don't eat, and if you don't eat, you don't live. Hunting has been a major way of sustenance, not just for food production but also for other resources. Animal fur, for example, can serve as clothing when the weather is too cold to go without it. We may be among the most intelligent species in the world, but we indeed aren't built the best for surviving in a perfect state of nature. With animal skins, we can thrive in temperatures well below what we'd typically be able to tolerate usually.

Before we begin, remember this: Nature is preserved. The world quickly turns into a concrete jungle, and hunters must protect the animals if we want to continue hunting. If we don't protect nature, who will? As a hunter, respect the world around you. You should revere the wilderness that provides you with the sustenance that keeps you going and honor and protect it from harm. Therefore, many states & places like Ontario make hunters go through a course before issuing any hunting licenses.

Following specific guidelines while hunting helps prevent the endangerment of wildlife. The rules we have out there keep everyone safe; they protect you from doing something dangerous and also protect nature from further strain than is sustainable. With the constant urbanization of remove wildlife land, we must protect what is left of it. After all, life is sacred, and even though we as hunters take it, we know we should preserve the species for future hunting. If we go all in and hunt them all to death, there would be nothing left for future hunts. Future generations wouldn't be able to rely on these wonderful natural resources to take care of themselves. As responsible hunters, we must preserve these animals for the future. To preserve the wildlife, many places require you to keep track of how many animals you hunt and to limit what you may target in many situations.

Caring for your kills is just as important as knowing how to hunt responsibly and sustainably. As soon as you get that kill, the clock ticks… You only have so long to field dress the kill before you risk contamination. The wilderness isn't exactly the cleanest place around, and as soon as the immune system stops working, you run into the danger of having the meat grow bacteria. Or, if you don't open the animal up the right way, you could unintentionally contaminate everything with the entrails or brain, both of which are supposed to be kept as far away from the meat as possible. You need to get it cleaned out safely and brought down to a safe temperature as soon as possible to reduce the risk of food-borne illnesses.

Everything about hunting hinges upon your reflexes and speeds. You'll need to respond and catch your prey as quickly as possible. You'll need to field dress quickly, typically in less than an hour, to prevent bacteria from taking hold. To be prepared, you'll need to also have the right equipment on hand for use at a moment's notice. (Tip: The quicker you field dress your meat and cool, it will dictate how good your meat will taste!)

≡ PREPARING FOR SAFE HUNTING

There are enough risks in hunting to feel you should take on new ones. Make sure that you always take the time to prepare for a safe hunting expedition, ensuring that you're in good physical shape to hunt, you're dressed for hunting, and familiarize yourself with the risks. If you're reading this book, there's a chance you're a complete newbie to hunting, so ensuring that you do nothing too risky will help to protect you in the long run.

PHYSICAL WELLNESS

To protect yourself, avoid hunting if you are not feeling well. This is a recipe for disaster as you could end up contracting a worse sickness. The body is more prone to illness when exposed to conditions that weaken the immune system some more. Take the precaution to keep yourself safe and avoid contracting infections and diseases that could worsen your sickness.

DRESS FOR SUCCESS

When you're out hunting, you expose yourself to many elements that you may need to consider. You might be, for example, out in the weather too cold or wet to get through without winter gear. Or, you could be somewhere that is hot and sunny, in which case you'll still need protection from the sun to prevent sunburn. There's always a risk of animal or insect bites in the forest, and ticks or other blood-sucking animals may be more than happy to take on the free meal if they see some bare skin.

Make sure that you cover your skin with appropriate clothing for the weather. If there are forecasts of rain or snow, make sure you have something waterproof that will help you continue to stay warm. You could also wear several layers, which you can remove or add on as the weather changes throughout the day. Shoes should be appropriate to walk through the terrain you've chosen as well. (Tip: To be a successful hunter, you need to be prepared for all elements of nature.)

Many hunting areas have regulations about wearing an orange vest for visibility to other people. Make sure that when you're hunting, you follow any regulatory laws. They're there to protect you and while it's a good idea to hide when you're hunting, remember that you don't want someone else to not see you because of your camouflage.

KNOW WARNING SIGNS IN NATURE

Avoid hunting animals that show any symptom of illness. If it's not running as fast as its legs will take it away from you, or it is not as alert as it should be, there is most likely something wrong with the animal. Sick animals could transmit zoonotic diseases to whoever handles or eats them. To prevent illness, make sure that you avoid these animals. If it isn't a challenge for you to hunt, it's probably too good to be true.

You may also want to consider looking out for signs of old, infected illnesses. If there is anything that doesn't look quite right on your kill, there could be a problem, and it's usually better to be safe than sorry. Anything that looks suspicious should be thoroughly examined, and the affected part of the meat should also be cut off to avoid the spread of any infection in the wound.

Suppose it's your first-time field dressing or handling game. In that case, you may not be acquainted with the inner structure of the animal you are hunting, but if you have the slightest sign that something is not right with the game you have hunted, consult someone more experienced than you are or consider disposing of the carcass. Things like blood clots unassociated with the hunting injury, offensive smell, suspicious muscular arrangement, and so on show that something is wrong with the animal.

TIPS FOR FIELD DRESSING SMALL GAME

When you finally get your kill, you're probably eager to ensure that you dress it appropriately. You want to make sure that you treat it well to enjoy the fruits of your labor. Field dress properly means recognizing when and how to make it happen quickly, so the meat is spared. You want to save as much of the meat as possible to avoid wasting the animal, so the sooner you catch onto the necessary actions you'll need to take, the better.

THE PROCESS

The process of field dressing isn't that hard. Especially when you have a smaller game, you rarely need to struggle too much. Your strength is typically enough to cut through skin and bones. Be even more careful—most tools that we use may be too large to use on small squirrels to gut them effectively. If you've never field dressed small game, it's relatively simple. You begin with skinning and gutting (or gutting and skinning in some situations). Then, you simply clean it out, and you're on your way.

Some animals will have a few more steps. Others will have a few less. Luckily for you, we'll be going through all the details, step by step, shortly.

Just remember, this isn't necessarily a clean or glamorous process. There will be blood. You may accidentally bust a gut at least once (we've all been there!). You'll find animals that don't look so good once you open them up. Just keep. Not all kills will be that great, and that's okay.

CLEAN IT QUICKLY

One of the most important rules is that you should clean and store your kill as quickly as possible. While some hunters may be fine tying their small game kills to their waists as they continue hunting, the meat will always taste the best when you clean it sooner. This will help you remove any nasty bacteria or other stinky parts sooner rather than later before they foul the meat. The meat can spoil much quicker if the innards are left intact longer. Even if you hunt in colder weather, you still need to clean it quickly. Think of it this way: you are trying to bring down the internal temperature of an animal that has a pelt or feathers designed to insulate it and keep it warm. The temperatures will not drop quickly enough for the meat to be good if you leave it intact, and the digestive enzymes will have the chance to taint the meat.

Most animals can be gutted immediately after you've reclaimed them. Even if you don't want to stop and strip feathers off your bird, you can still remove the guts and let the cooling start. Rabbits and squirrels are easy enough to break down all at once. Just get it over with and be on your way. Your meat will taste the best.

AVOID GUT BUSTING

Gut-busting happens when you nick the digestive system and everything in it comes spilling out. It smells awful and can taint the taste of your meat if you let it. It could even allow for passing food borne bacteria and disease if you're not careful. E. coli and other dangerous pathogens can be found in the guts and can cause problems, which can be made even worse if you cannot keep the meat cool enough.

REMOVE HAIRS

If you are rough or messy with the meat that you're cleaning, you might end up with tiny hairs in the meat after you've skinned them. You could run the meat under running water if you can, or you could burn them off with a lighter, torch, or burner. The best way to avoid the problem is to be more mindful as you skin your meat simply.

POP JOINTS INSTEAD OF CUTTING BONE

Some people like to try cutting right through the bones of their animals. However, this is a dangerous practice. Bones can splinter and leave small, dangerous pieces in the meat that are consumed. Bone shards could also poke straight through vacuum bags if you're not careful. Rather than cutting through bone, make it a point to pop the joint. This will allow you to separate it, breaking nothing, keeping the meat safe from bone shards.

AVOID BRAINS AND ENTRAILS

While field dressing, keep the entrails and brain matter of the animal away from the meat itself. Therefore, from the start, aim for a clean shot. Killing the animal with one shot is more humane and less messy. Shooting the animal around the abdomen could cause a lot of mess during the process of field dressing.

WASHING TOOLS

Wash your tools, but do not wash the animal itself. Suppose you've done everything right while field dressing; you wouldn't have to clean the meat. Washing the dressed game exposes it to contamination. Just place the meat in a bag and store them in an ice-packed cooler to preserve it.

Ensure you wash your hands thoroughly with water and soap, especially if you touch the animal's innards. Your hands are your most valuable tools, after all!. Wash the tools you used, wash the surface you worked on. Everything must be washed with soap and water and properly disinfected. Add bleach to the water you use for washing up afterward. The bleach serves as a disinfectant on the go. Just be mindful never to drink water that has had bleach added to it.

☰ FIELD DRESSING SMALL GAME

Once you've got your kill secured, you will need to process it quickly to keep it from spoiling too quickly. This all begins with removing the guts, and sometimes the skin, from the carcass to preserve the edible areas. Processing is often something that people think will be difficult, but it's pretty simple to figure out what you're doing once you know what you're doing. You just need to know what it will take to make it happen.

The first few times you process something, it might not be pretty, but pretty doesn't matter when it tastes good! The most important thing to remember is to keep your meat clean at all times. This is non-negotiable and will always be the most essential part of the process. Once you've gotten the kill, it's time to clean it to enjoy the fruits of your labor later.

☰ EASY 7 STEP SQUIRREL FIELD DRESSING GUIDE

Squirrels aren't the first animal that people often think of when talking about hunting. They're small and somewhat nutty after a life of eating nuts. In some areas, hunting squirrels is regulated, so make sure that you are always aware of the restrictions placed in your area.

Field dressing squirrels should be done as soon as possible. The animal should be opened up to cool down as soon as it is picked up. Typically, you skin squirrels before you gut them because once you've gutted a squirrel, it doesn't have enough meat to keep it stable enough for the skinning process.

Work in a clean environment as possible to prevent contamination. This will be the first step of every single animal you learn how to dress.

Keep in mind that while traditionally, people create a hole in the hide and pull in opposite directions, because squirrels have tougher hides, they shed hair that gets all over the meat during this process. Instead, you can use a method of skinning that comes with a quick pull. In just seven steps, using a squirrel skinner, you can remove the hide quickly and easily. A squirrel skinner is a piece of metal with three slots where you can put the back legs to skin it easily.

1 Begin by placing the legs in a squirrel skinner, keeping the back facing toward you.

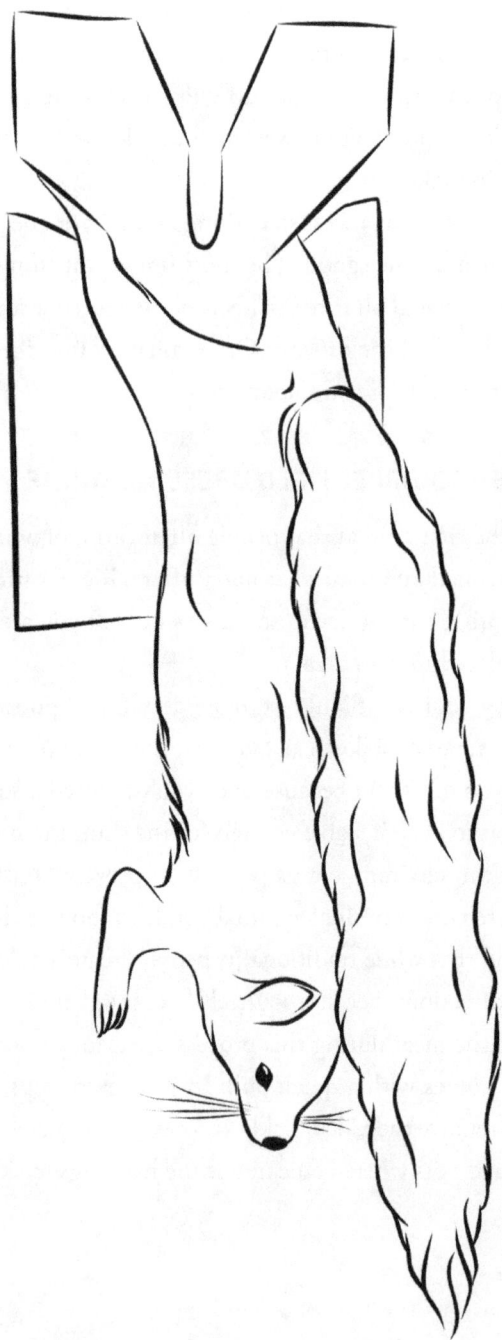

2 Then, remove some of the hair at the base of the tail. This is so you can make a small incision at the base of the tail, cutting between the tail bone joints, then twisting to sever it.

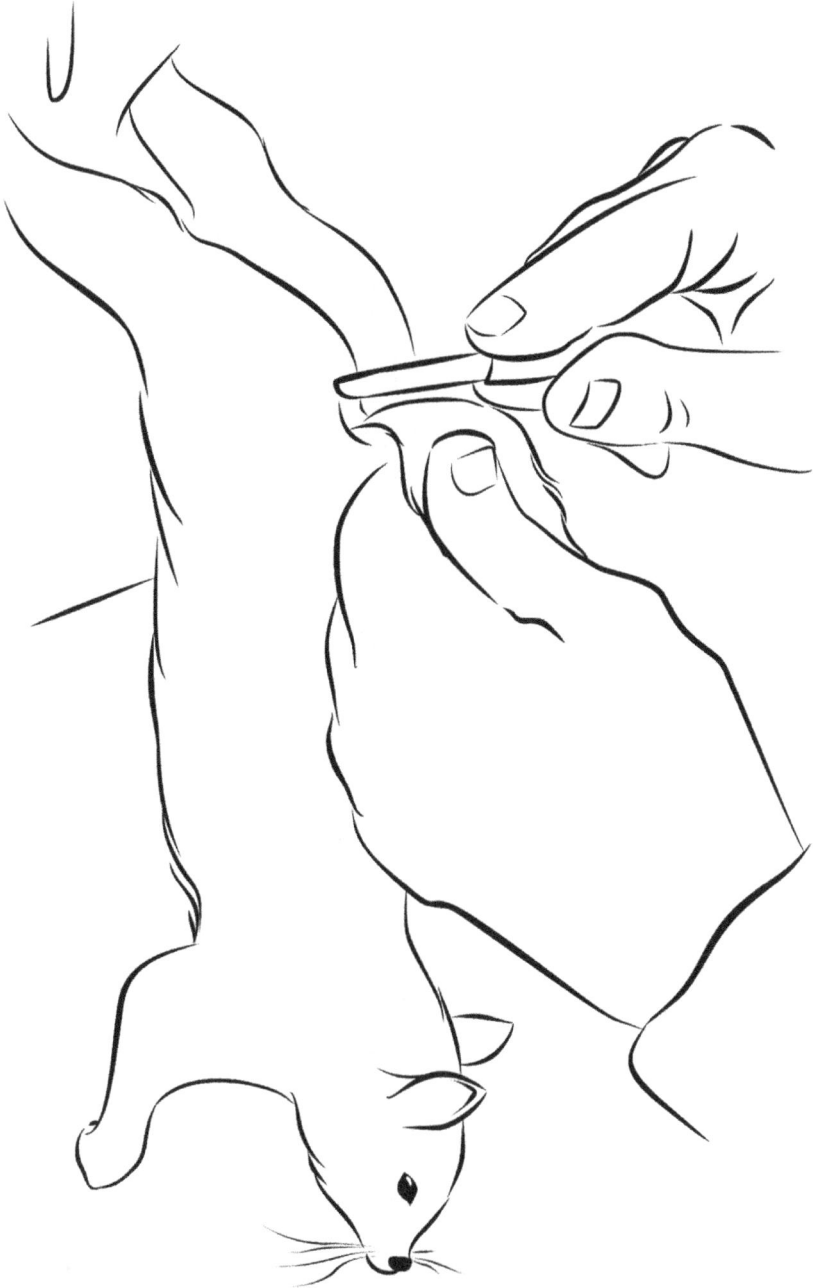

3 Skin down the squirrel's back slowly and carefully for a few inches.

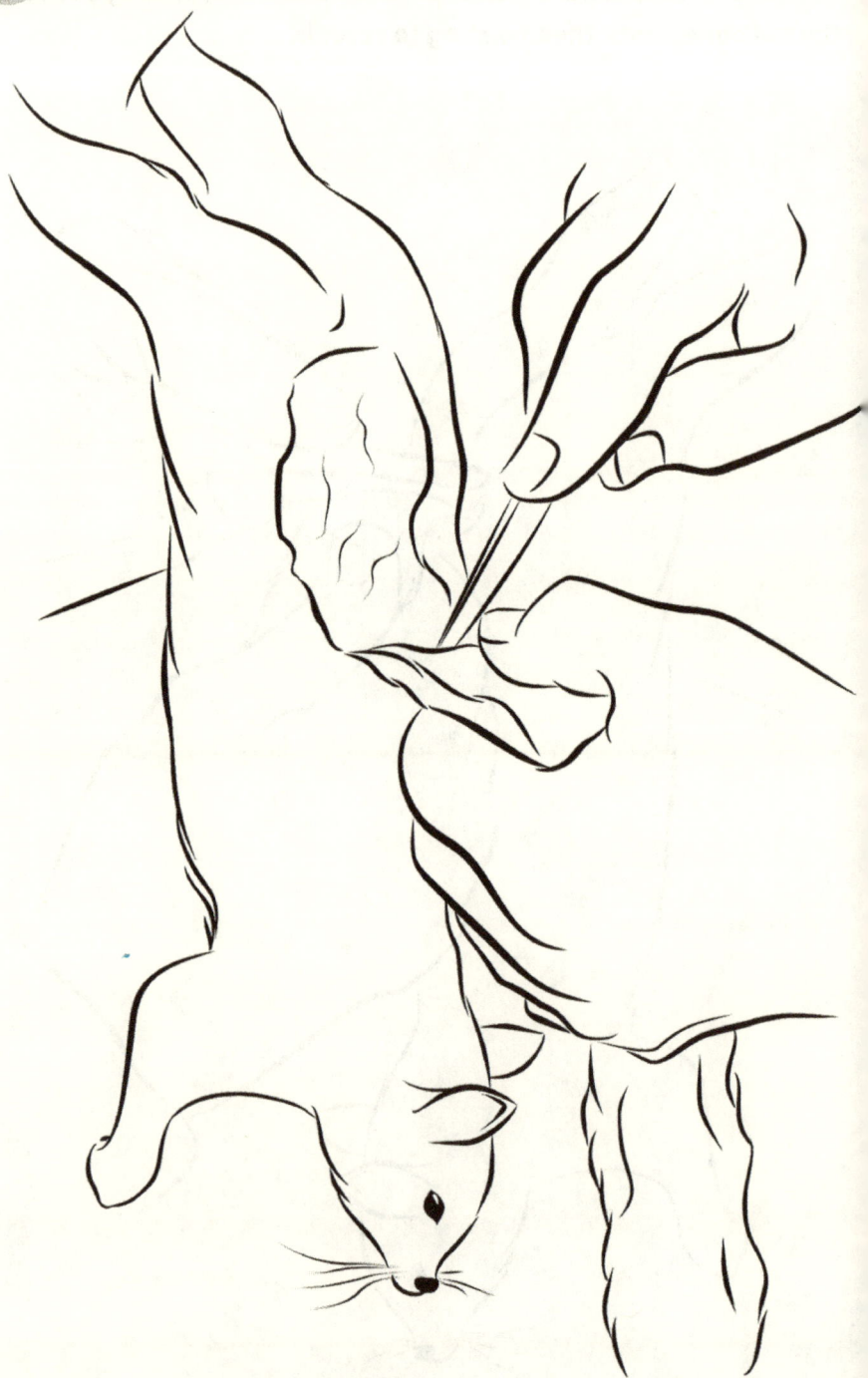

4 Remove the squirrel from the skinner, then grab the back legs. Step down on the tail of the squirrel and pull it up. The front of the hide should then pull down past the front legs.

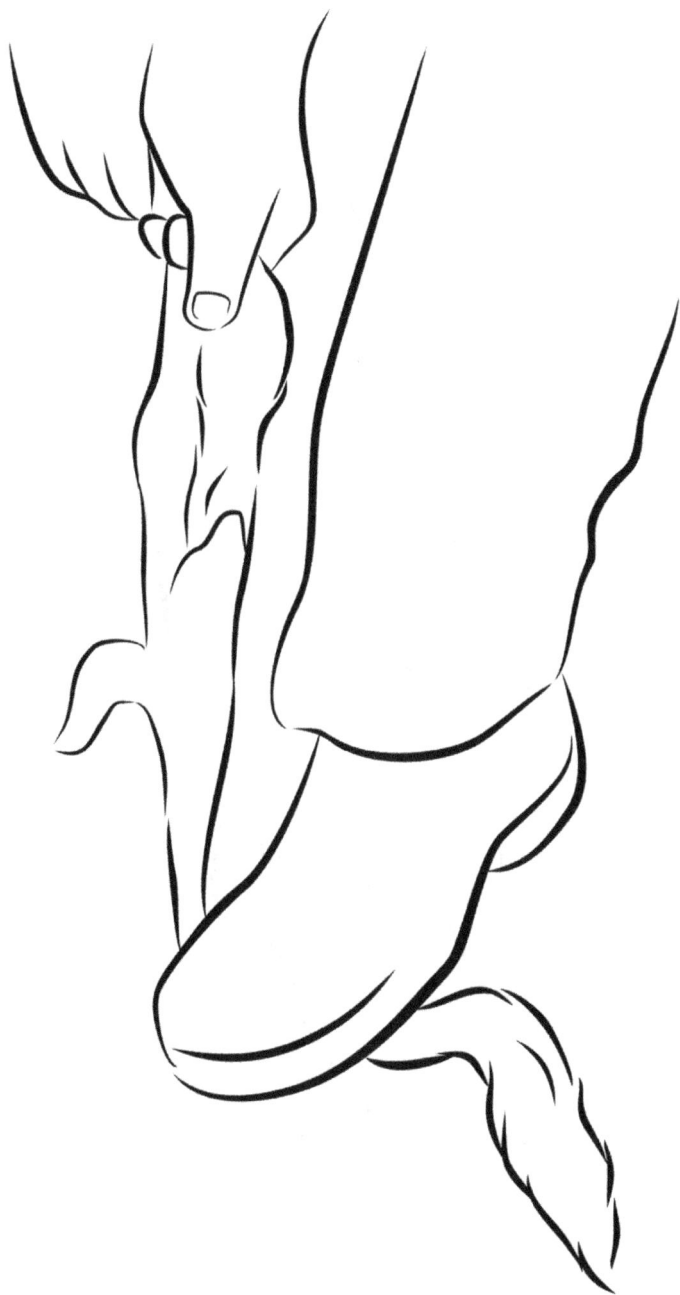

5 Keeping the tail beneath your foot, hold the skin attached to the belly, and pull it up toward the rear hide past the rear legs.

6 Pull down as far as you can on the hide in the front and rear legs. Most of the heads should be exposed at this point.

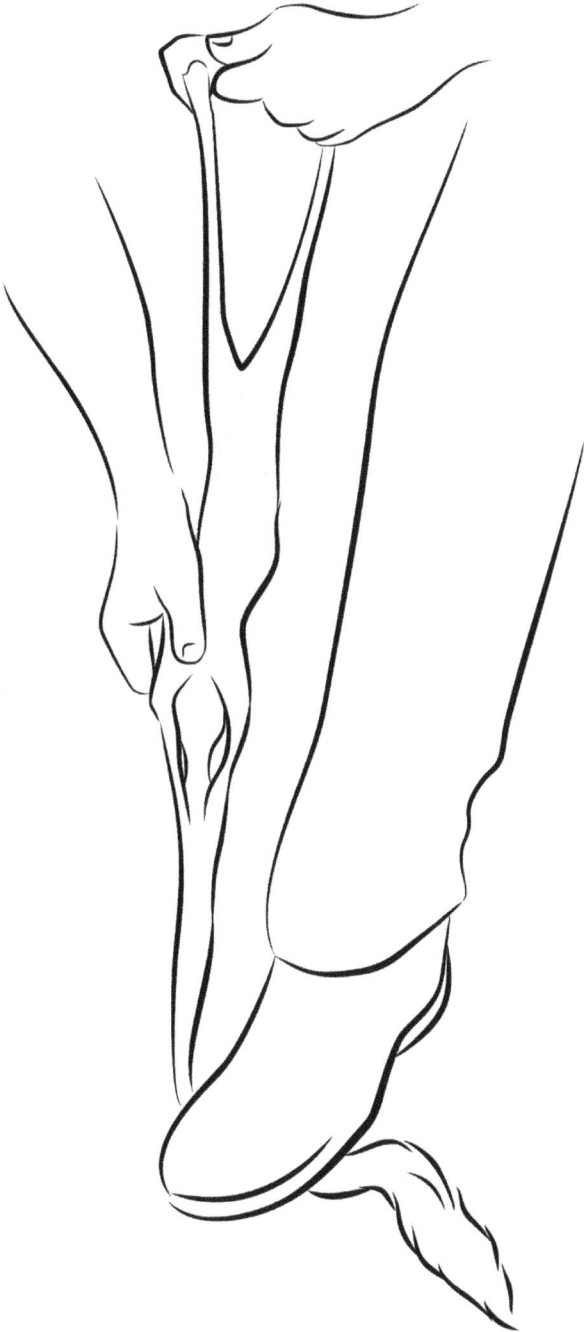

7 Put the squirrel back in the skinner and gut the carcass, then remove the legs with a pair of shears.

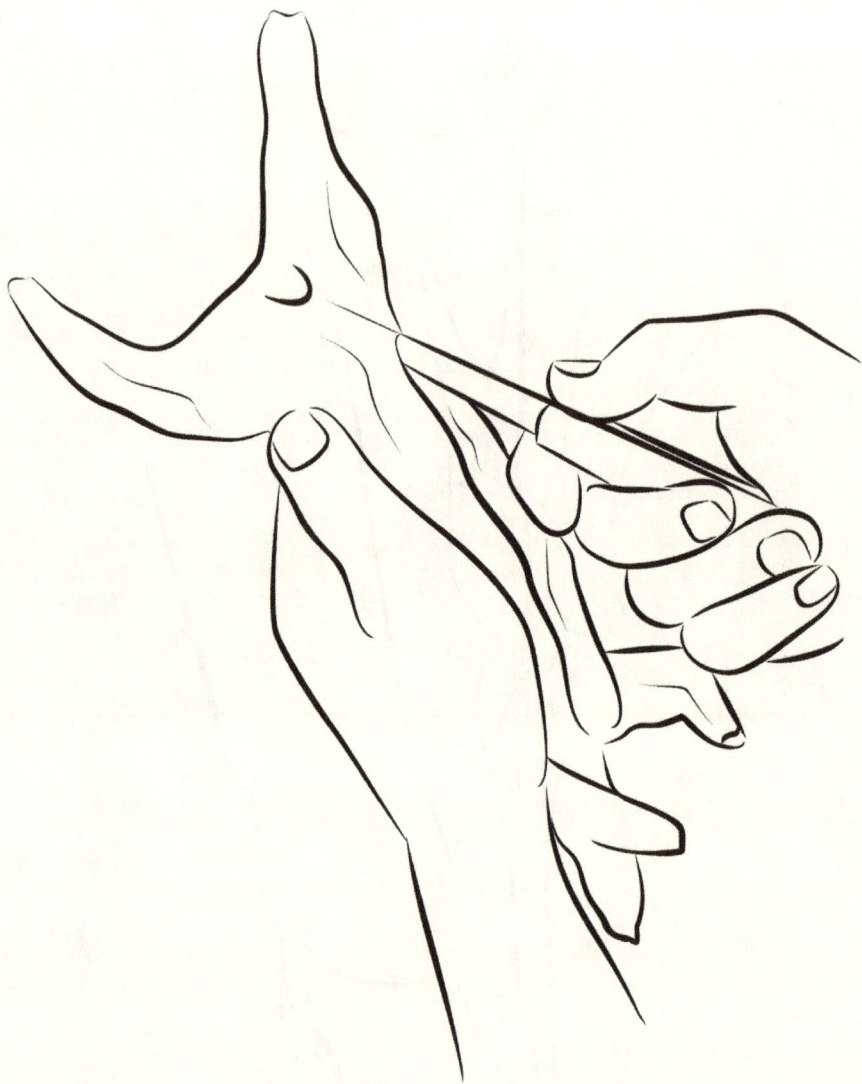

SIMPLE 7 STEP RABBIT FIELD DRESSING GUIDE

Rabbits and hares are easier to handle when compared with squirrels because they're bigger and have more meat on their bones. While squirrels are too delicate to skin after gutting, rabbits are typically field dressed with removing the organs first and then skinning after. Rabbit meat can be a great treat. Wild rabbit is almost chicken-like, sweetish and gamey, and maybe lean as well.

In just seven simple steps, be able to remove everything from your rabbit or hare to have it ready to enjoy it when you want it. You'll need to have game shears, a knife, water, and a garbage bag on hand. And as always, you'll want to remove the skin and field dress it as quickly as possible to cool the meat.

1 Begin by removing the feet at the ankles and the head of your catch.

2 To remove the skin, make a small horizontal cut on the back. Space needs to be enough to insert your fingers and stretch and separate the skin from the meat. Dunk it in the water here.

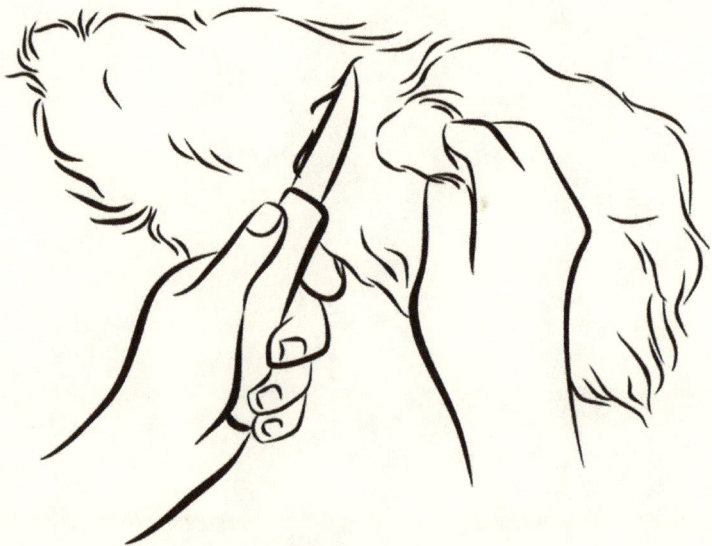

3 From that space, grab the hide at the edge of each slit and pull it down and off. The hide will slide off the animal as you pull at it. The whole thing should come clean.

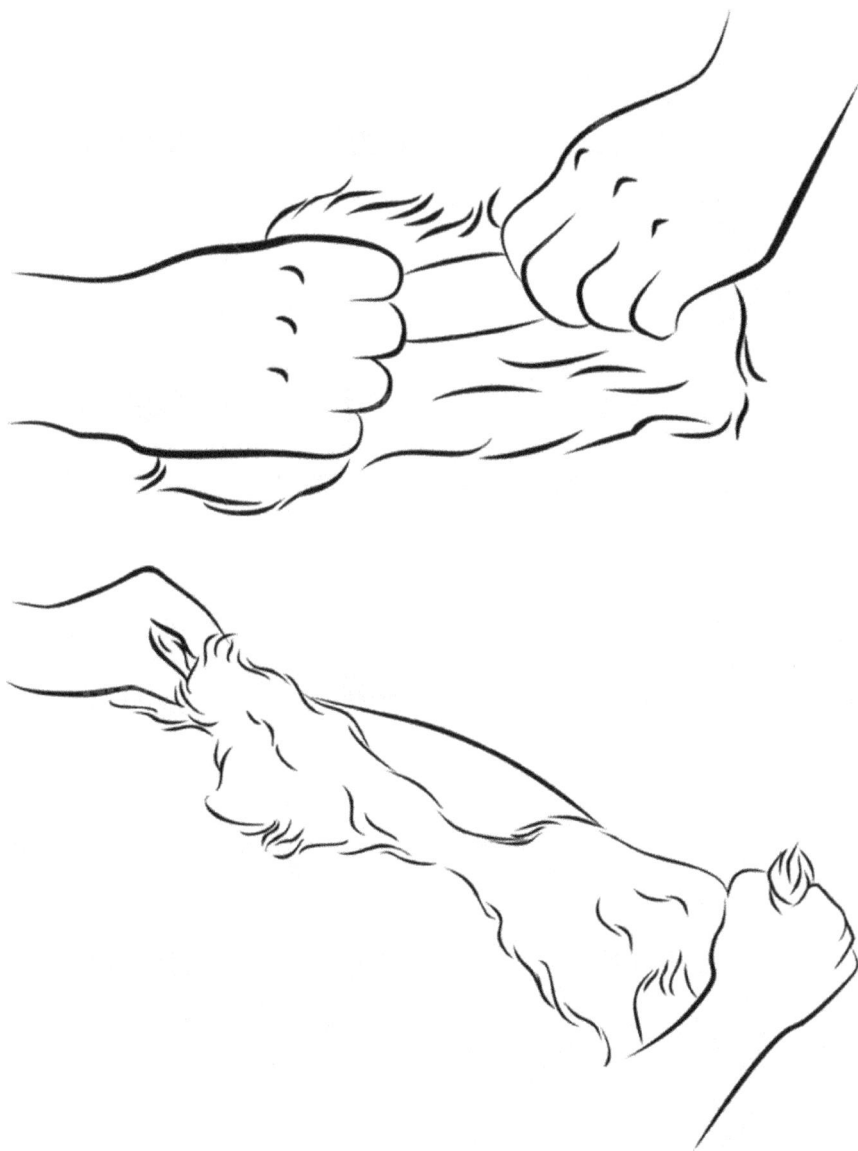

4 Open the belly from the neck to the anus, carefully avoiding the entrails.

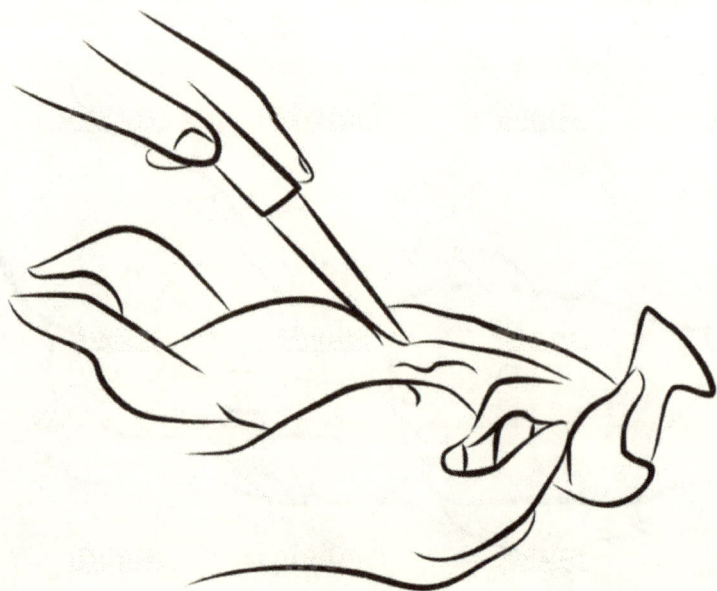

5 Grab the heart and lungs, pulling backward. The entrails should come with it.

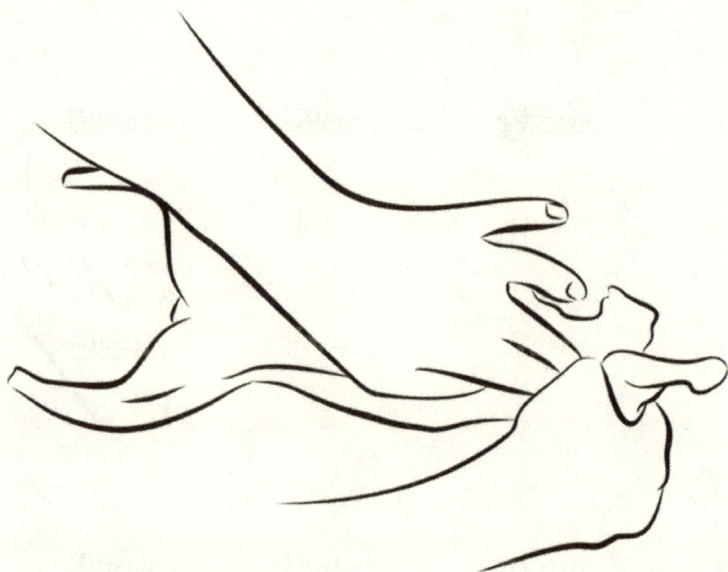

6 Use the knife to remove the hindquarters from the pelvis, front quarters, and backstrap.

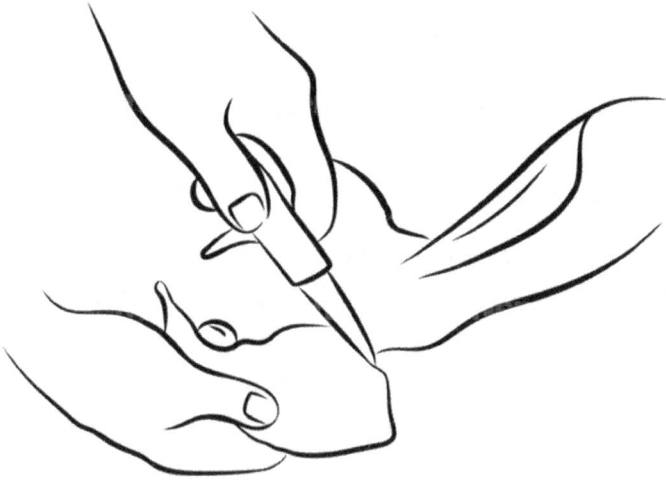

7 Finished Piece: Rinse the meat off to remove blood, dirt, and hair, and then either freeze it for later or prepare it for cooking now. You now have a backstrap, thighs, and front legs.

☰ 30 SECOND GROUSE/PARTRIDGE FIELD DRESSING GUIDE

If you haven't had grouse or partridge before, you're in for a treat. They are tender and delicious. If you like poultry, you'll probably like grouse/partridge as well. Cleaning grouse/partridges are incredibly simple. You can do it in seconds when you get good at it, making it highly efficient. All you need to do is ensure that you're on the right track. This method is highly effective for most small game birds.

1 Place the bird on the ground on its back. Stand on either side of the bird's wings, with the tail end by your heels and the head facing forward. Using your feet to put pressure where the wing joins the body, grab the feet firmly in your hands.

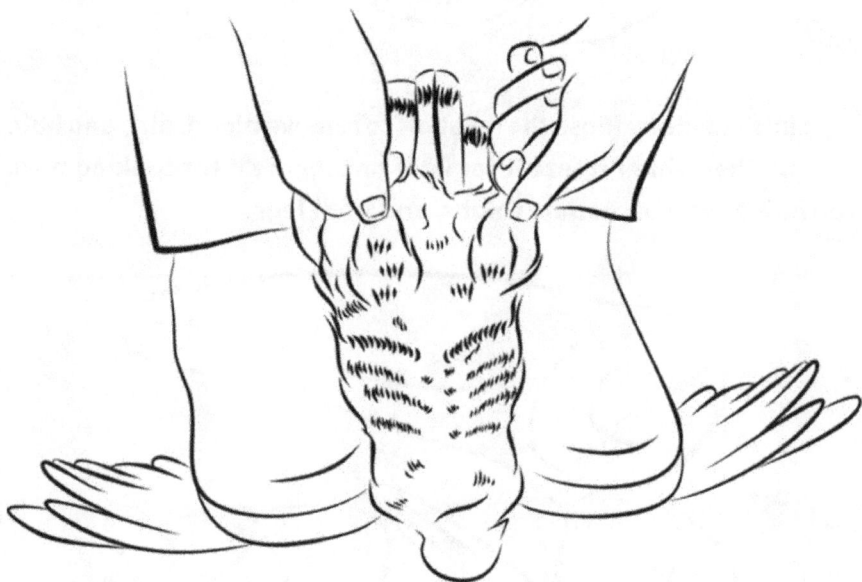

2 Using firm, even pressure, pull the legs up and away from the body. Typically, this is easier with fresher kills. You're then left with the head, entrails, and wings on the ground with the breast while holding the legs in your hand. Use your finger to remove the head and entrails from the breast, starting at the top.

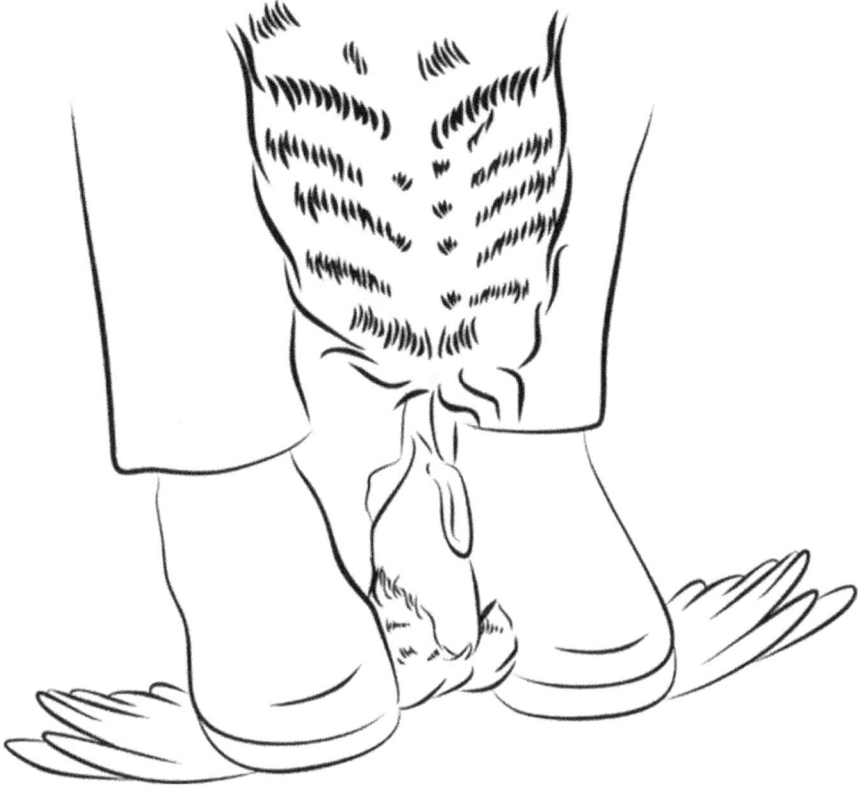

3 Finally, you need to remove the wings. Do so with a sharp knife, or twist and snap them away. Remove any feathers left behind and wash thoroughly under cold running water. Freeze immediately or eat within the next few days.

☰ 7-STEP DOVE/PHEASANT/QUAIL FIELD DRESSING GUIDE

Quail can be a great meal if you can find them, but they've slowly become more complex and harder to find. Rather than just breasting the quail, consider removing the feathers, cleaning the birds, and using them whole. You'll be in for a great treat when you do! These birds are pretty small, so you'll want to be mindful of how you use them. Try to make the most out of the meat while you can.

If you've landed a pheasant on the table, you're going to have a delicious meal! The wild pheasant is gamey, aromatic, and lean. They are small, so if you're cooking a meal for several people, you'll probably want a few birds by. It can be a great treat. Keep in mind that in many places, pheasants are regulated, and you are only allowed to hunt males to prevent overhunting or removing valuable females from the reproduction pool.

Alternatively, if you get some dove on the table, you'll have a mild, flavorful meal that may not be as juicy as pheasant but tastes great. This is especially the case if you get morning doves in your area, providing lean, dark meat that tastes amazing. (Tip: It may be dry, but you can usually keep it moist just by adding bacon. Bacon makes everything delicious!)

Whether you got a dove, pheasant, or quail, the field dressing process is more or less the same. You just have to follow a few simple steps to clean it out and prepare it to eat.

1 Start by removing the head of your bird. This is optional, but ensure that the bird is dead rather than stunned before you move on with the rest of the steps.

2 Next, you need to remove the wings from the bird. The wings and bones are connected to the breast, so you want to ensure they're broken before removal, or you could tear the breast. Grab the bone as close to the body as you can, then twist and snap the wing bone. This will probably rip the skin away as you remove the wing.

3 Take your headless and wingless bird and hold it in your non-dominant hand on its back, with the neck pointing down. Grab the back firmly, with your thumb underneath the base of the tail, as close to the body as you can.

4 Take your dominant hand and use your thumb to find the lip of the breast under the chest. Use your thumbs to push and force their ways through the body cavity, pulling the breast away from the back. The two pieces should hinge near the neck as they separate.

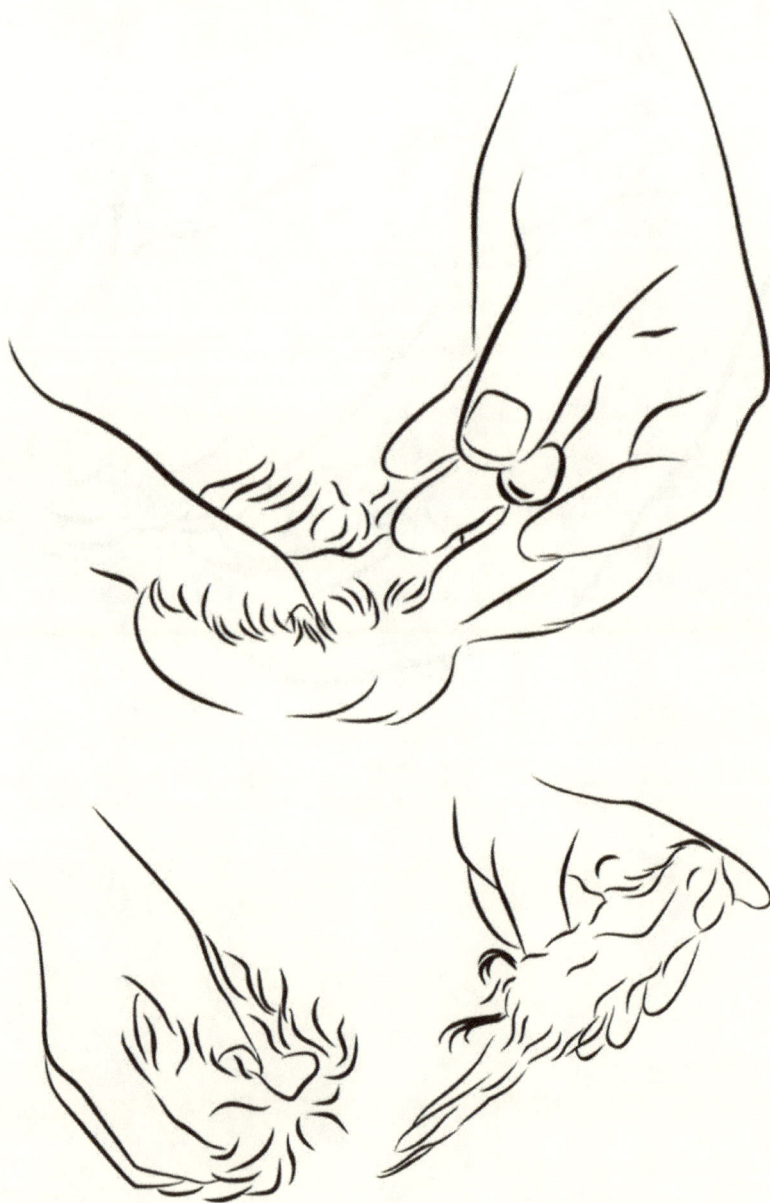

5 You can secure the heart and gizzard, which can provide additional nutrition for you to enjoy. As you pluck these out, slice open the gizzard and remove the liner and the bird's last meal. Clean them up and save them to cook with the bird.

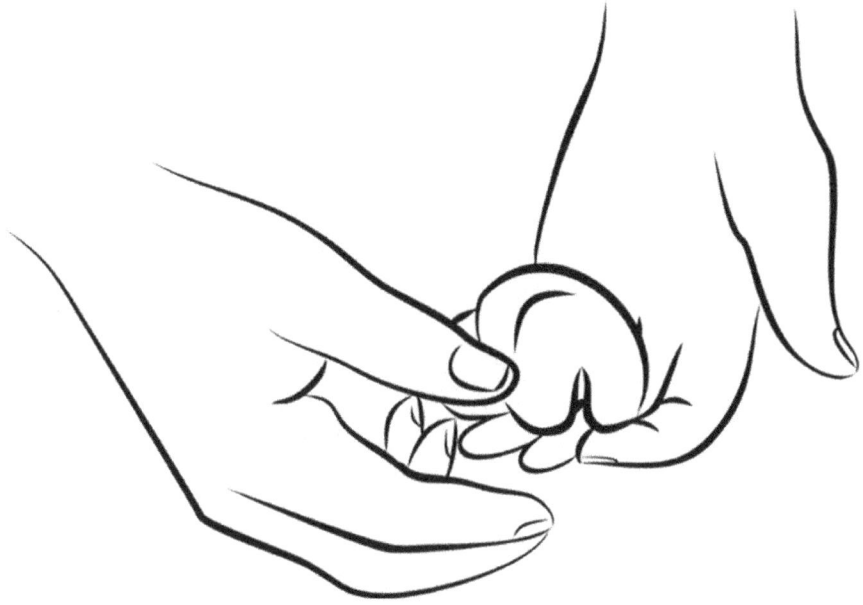

6 Next comes defeathering and removing the breast. You can usually pull the breast away from the rest of the bird easily at this stage, and feathers and skin can be pulled away easily using your fingers.

7 Clean the meat thoroughly at this point and make sure that the meat isn't infested with anything. Worms or infections could taint the meat. Then, cook thoroughly and enjoy. Any extra scraps can bait for future hunts or be disposed of properly.

≡ DUCK

1 **Position the duck, so it is on its back, feet directed toward you. With a knife, remove the wings, cutting at the joints to separate them. Pull the wings so you can separate the joint, then cut the connective tissue away.**

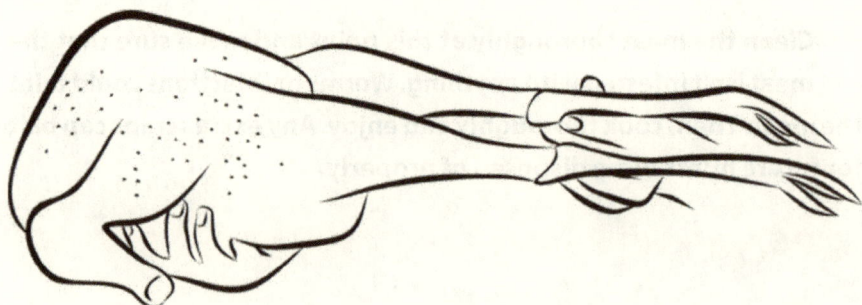

2 Remove the legs by creating an incision all around the large joint, only cutting through the skin. Then, twist the joint a few times to loosen the tendons, remove and pull. The foot should detach with the tendons to create tender thigh meat.

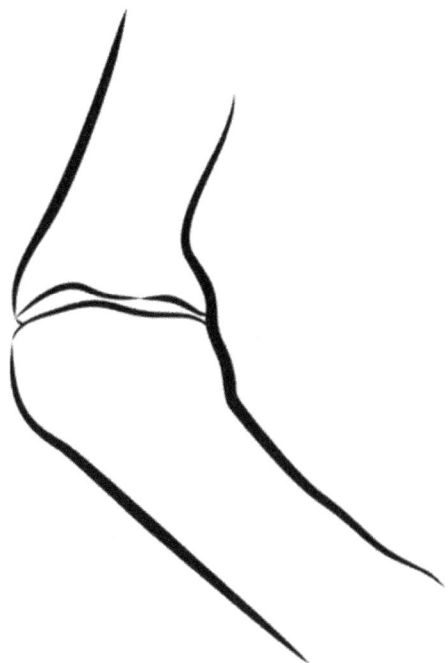

3 Leave the head-on, for now, to hold on to as you pluck feathers. To do so, pinch up a few feathers between your thumb and forefinger, pulling quickly to remove them. Pinch a few at a time to ensure you get cleaner skin without ripping the skin.

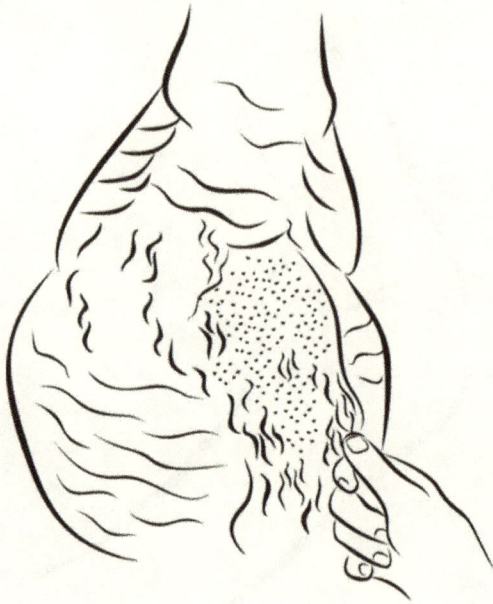

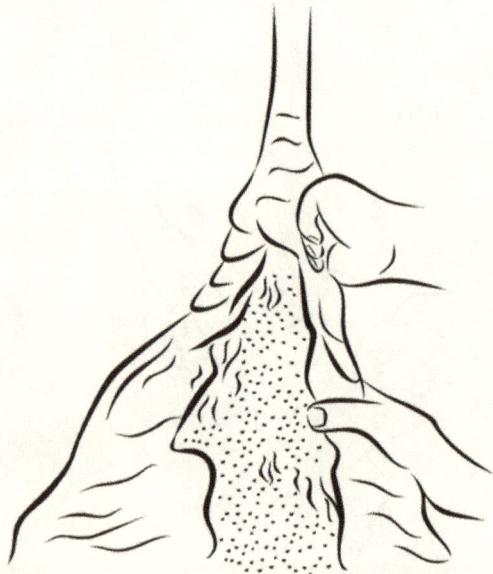

4 When you've removed all the feathers, place the duck down, back up, and tail toward you. Take your knife and create a slit from the base of the back and above the duck's vent. You want to slice through the vertebrae to open the duck. Free the tail and hold the duck, facing up.

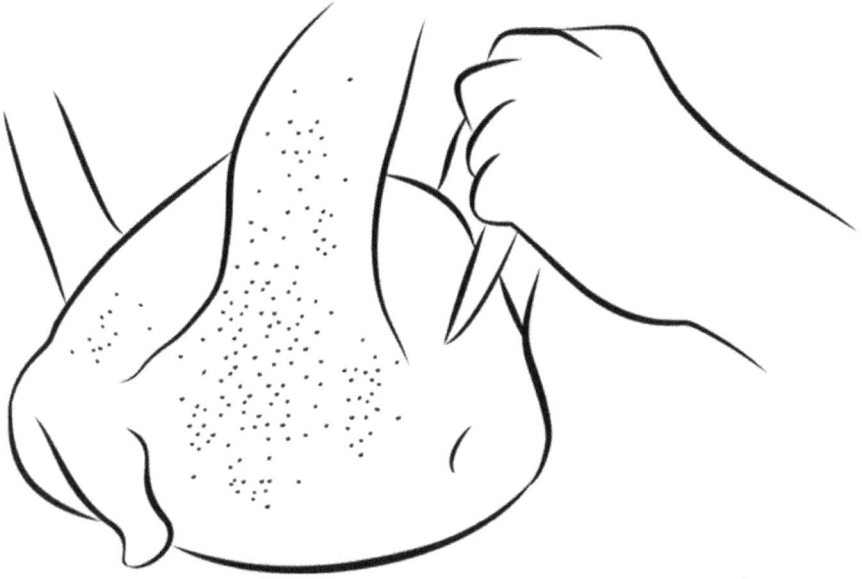

5 Cut carefully, inserting your knife gently into the body cavity, and cut away from you, from the tail end to the neck.

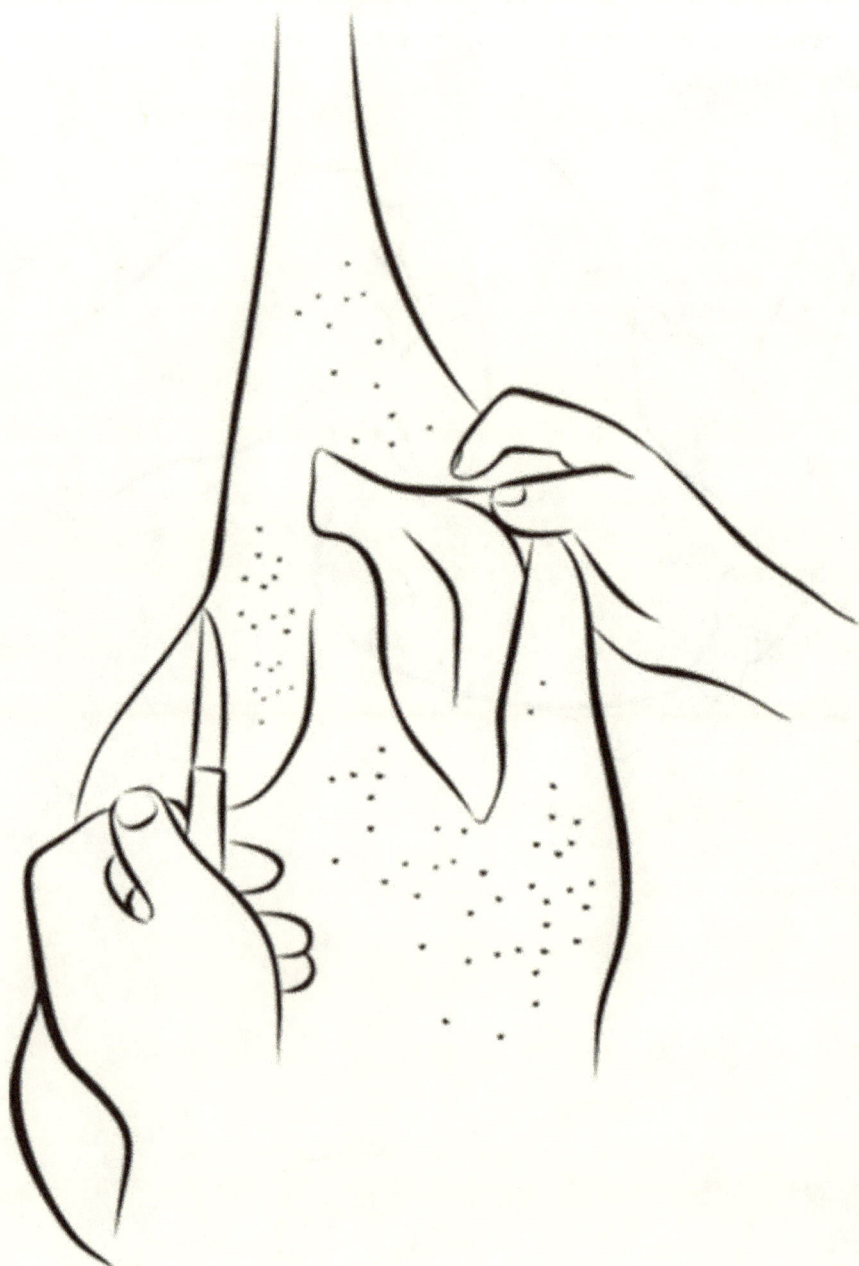

6 Remove the organs now, gently removing them starting at the neck side and working your way down. Start with the windpipe, then the lungs and diaphragm. Loosen the intestines and remove, rinse out the duck, and store until you're ready to eat it.

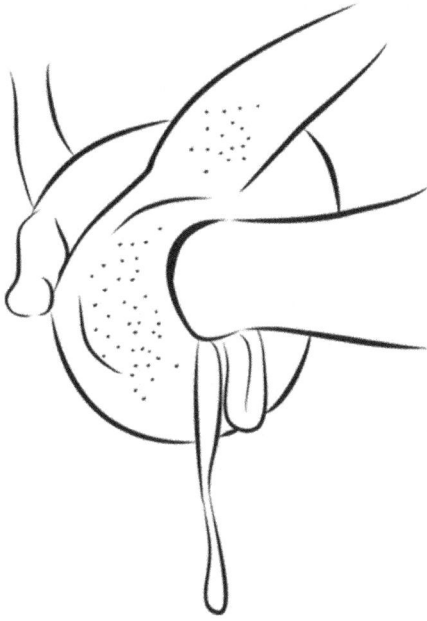

☰ TURKEY/GEESE FIELD DRESSING GUIDE

Wild turkeys in areas like Ontario are a unique breed of animals with distinctive sexual dimorphism that can be readily spotted. However, turkey wasn't always available to hunt. The wild turkey was hunted to extinction in the area and was reintroduced into the wild to repopulate. Because of the shaky status of the birds, hunting is regulated heavily, and people are only allowed to kill a certain amount of wild turkeys, with the annual allowance varying from year to year with the population. Typically, after mating has already passed during spring, male turkeys can be hunted, with females off-limits to encourage an increased population.

It is easy to spot females when hunting. The male wild turkey has black-colored tips on the end of its breast and side feathers, while the females have brown-colored feather tips around its breast and side feathers. The feathers on the chest of the male turkey are also longer than those on the female body, and the male turkeys make a lot more noise than their female counterparts. The male wild turkey is called a tom, while the female is known as a hen.

Many hunters advocate for keeping the skin on these birds—removing it is to remove delicious fat and flavor that can crisp up into something extraordinary if you let it cook. When you take care of a large bird, the first step is to pluck first before gutting, as otherwise, you may struggle to clean around the incision. Follow these simple steps.

1. Start by hanging your bird up by the neck. This will give you access to the whole thing all around, allowing the next several steps to be much easier.

2. Slowly remove the feathers, just a few at a time, tugging up and away from the bird to get them out of the skin.

3. Be mindful not to tear the skin, especially near the breast. It is the most fragile there, and you want the breast skin intact if you intend to roast your bird whole.

4. Continue to pluck, mindful that the most difficult parts will be the wing bones and the armpit area beneath the wing.

5. When you've removed all the feathers, you can then gut the bird entirely. Doing so while it's still hanging makes it easier. Create the gutting incision at the cloaca, and then slice toward the point of the breastbone.

6. Reach your hand into the cavity, pushing your hand to the wind-pipe. You'll need a firm grasp to bring the guts out without spilling their contents.

7. Keep the heart, liver, and gizzard.

8. Then, remove the breast sponge on turkeys. This is a collection of fatty tissue that sits above the breastbone and underneath the crop. To remove this, you'll need to cut up each side of the wishbone through the skin.

9. Next, slice the sack of fat away and leave behind the clean meat.

10. Remove the bird's head next. The wings can be left if you've completely plucked them. If they're not fully plucked, make sure you leave at least the first major joint intact, and you can cut beyond that, as there's very little usable meat in the second and third pieces of the wing, anyway.

11. Remove the legs, cutting around the joint where the rubbery scales meet the skin.

12. Snap the joint in half, and it should crack like a stick. Then, cut the tendons free. It's better to snap and remove the joint this way as sharp pieces of bone can pierce vacuum-seal bags if you decide to break down your kill further.

1 MINUTE BULLFROG FIELD DRESSING GUIDE

Many people don't hunt bullfrogs. However, other people simply don't like the idea of eating them, but they're missing out! These can be delicious meals that most people overlook. They're commonly served in restaurants in the south, France, Asia, and just about anywhere else where frogs can be found. However, especially the West Coast of the US has overlooked this delicious opportunity for plentiful meals.

Bullfrogs are invasive species in many places, so hunting them does the native species a favor. Once you've caught and killed a frog, you can then gut and clean it, enjoying the delicious meat. Most of the meat is found in the legs, so usually, people forgo worrying about the rest of them. The skin doesn't taste very good either, so you'll want to remove it.

Before you get started, you'll want to have a few tools on hand—shears, pliers, water, a sharp knife, and somewhere to dispose of the scraps left behind. Then, you can follow these steps.

1 Begin by removing the feet. It's easier to skin them when this is done.

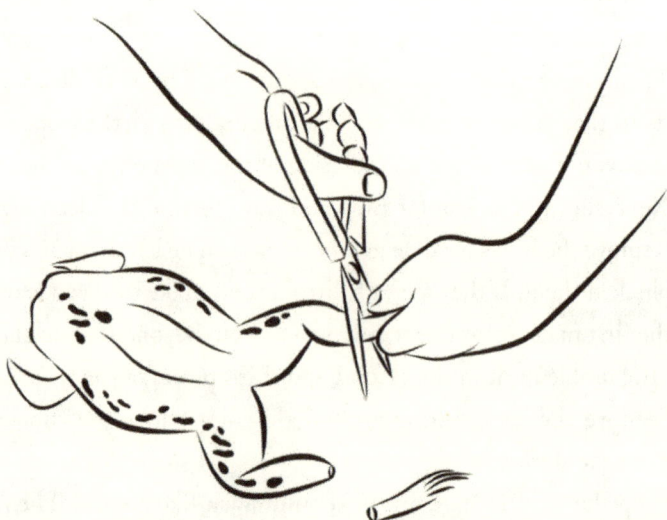

2 Slice the skin around the frog's waist. You can use either the kitchen shears or the knife, depending on what works best for you.

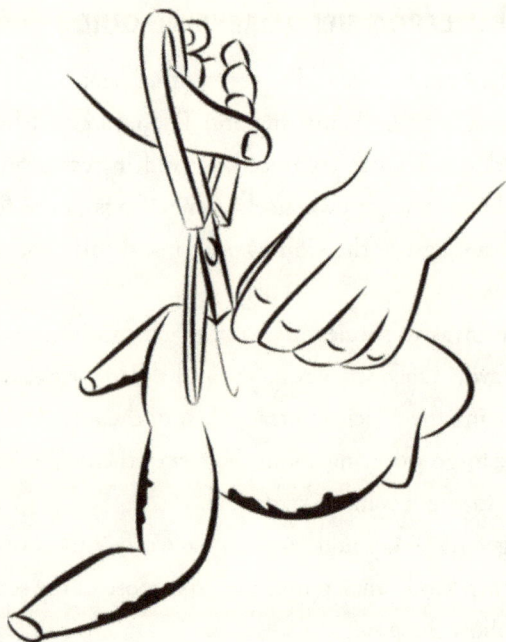

3 When the skin's been cut all the way around, the next step is easy. You'll use one hand to hold the top of the frog firmly. Then, take the pliers to grab the loose skin and yank the skin off, like you're pulling off a pair of pants.

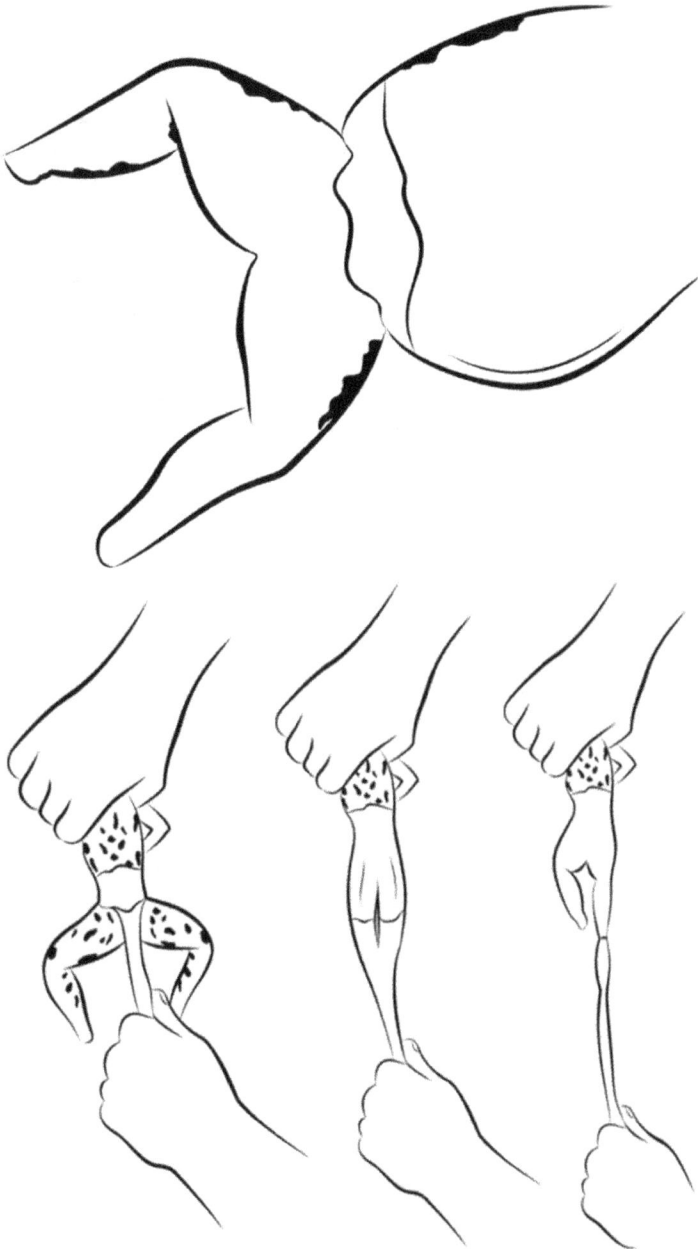

4 With the skin removed, use a pair of shears to chop off the legs like a pair right at the waist. Then, chop again to separate the legs into two pieces. You can also trim off any bits that look like organs kept on the leg slide when cutting.

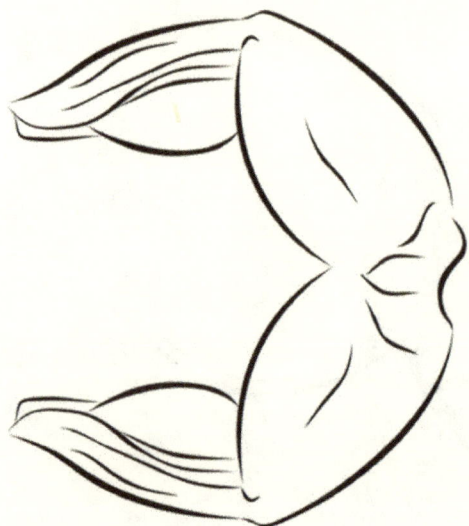

☰ SNAPPING TURTLE FIELD DRESSING GUIDE

If you get your hands on a snapping turtle (preferably the tail end so it can't bite you!), you've got a delicious meal, especially if you tenderize it and enjoy it in a delicious recipe. When you catch a snapping turtle, you're able to eat something tasty that most people will never bother enjoying. It's almost like being part of an exclusive club, knowing that everyone else is missing out because it's not traditionally eaten anymore.

Snapping turtles can be difficult to skin simply because they've got that massive shell on them, but if you can learn to do so effectively, you'll be in for a treat, and if you live somewhere, these are plentiful, you'll have even more to enjoy. Follow these simple steps to prepare your own.

1 **Start by finding a snapper yourself. You'll be able to do this in the wild if they're native to your area. Just keep them by their tail end to keep yourself safe. They pack quite a punch or, rather, bite.**

2 When you've got your turtle, stand on its shell to hold it in place to smash the head inwards toward the shell. This stuns the turtle so you can then continue the process. To kill it, you'll need to remove its head, slicing from the throat, through the spine, and then remove the head. This quickly kills it.

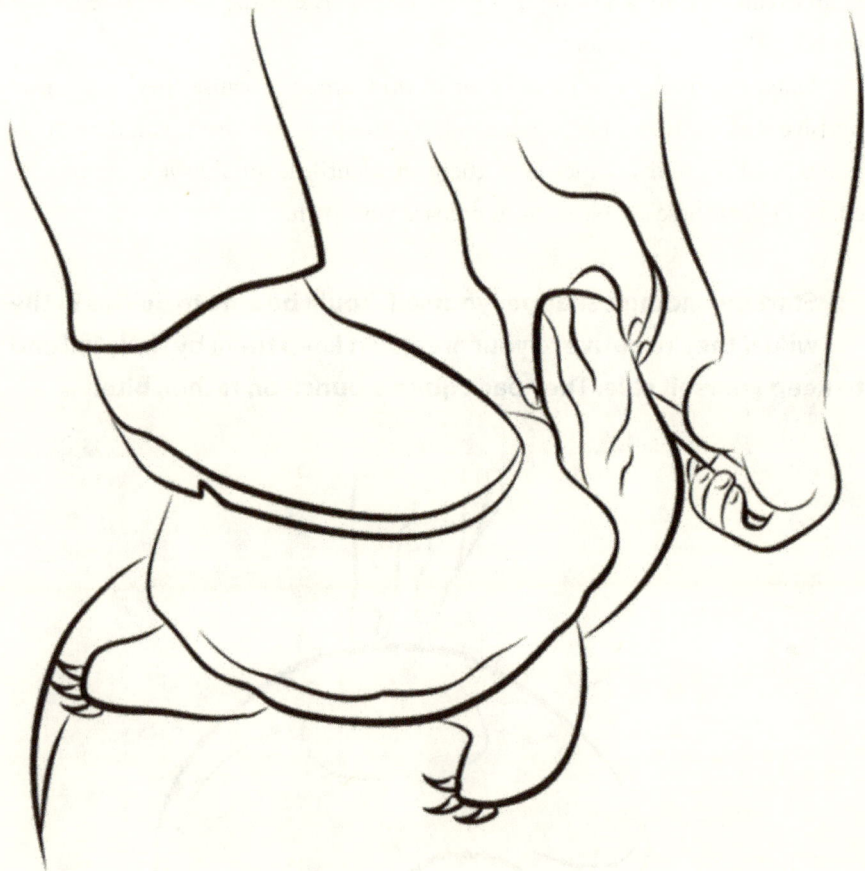

3 The easiest way to clean the turtle is to have it held in place. Prepare a plank of wood with a long nail through the center. Then, with the point of the nail through the wood and facing up, drive the turtle onto the nail to hold it in place. Start by removing the feet. You'll find the joints an inch behind the claws.

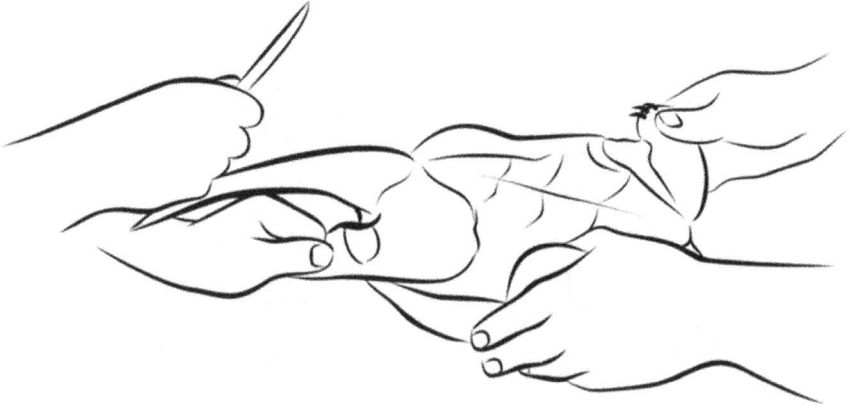

4 Next, you need to remove the shell. To do this, you'll need to cut through the center of the plate to the vent. Use a sharp, strong knife, plus a wooden baton if necessary to push it through. Cut down the center, then cut the perimeter to remove it.

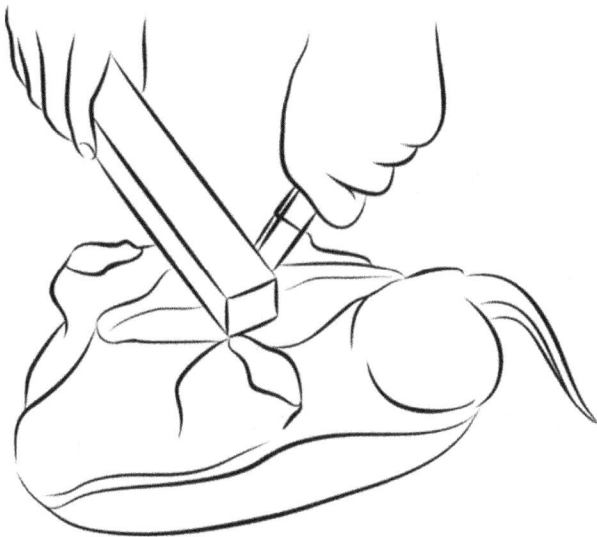

5 Start skinning the turtle from the inside out. Be mindful when you start because the front shoulder blade is near the shell. You don't want to cut too quickly and have your knife rebound out. Let the knife feel its way through slowly as you go.

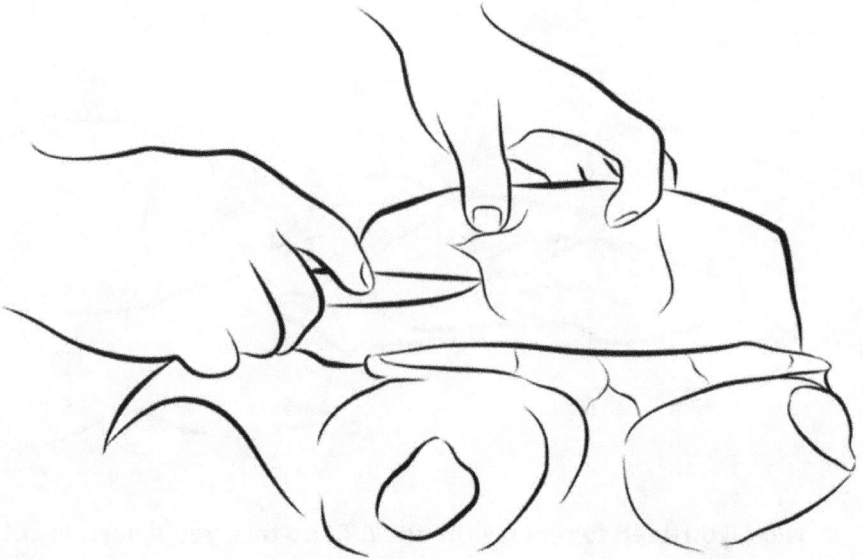

6 Then work around the legs to remove the skin. When the skin is removed, use a knife to remove the feet, slicing through the line under the shell and pulling it off.

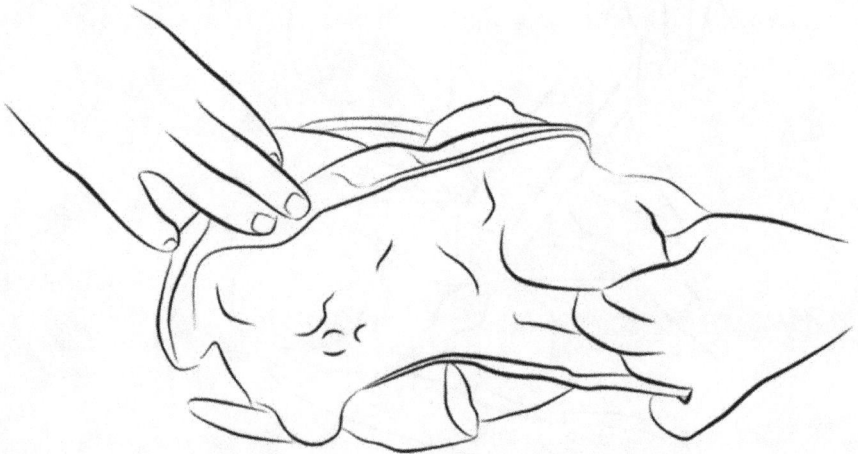

7 Pull-on, the tail, using the knife to remove the meat from the backbone.

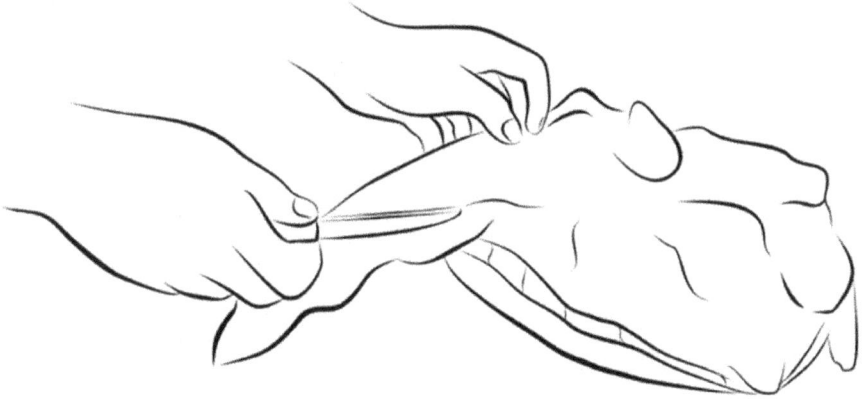

8 Pull out the meat as you cut. You may also find eggs as you do so, and those are edible as well.

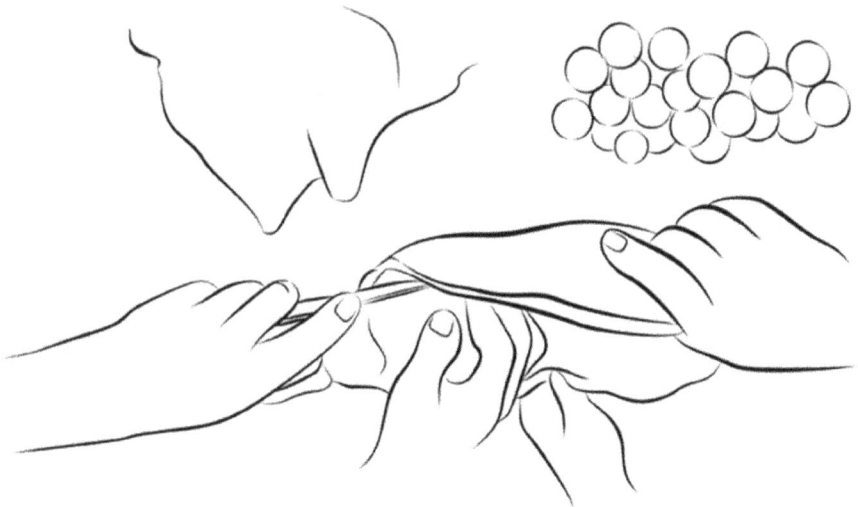

9 Finish scraping all meat out.

10 Meat can be broken down further or deboned if desired. Soak in water overnight for a day or two before cooking.

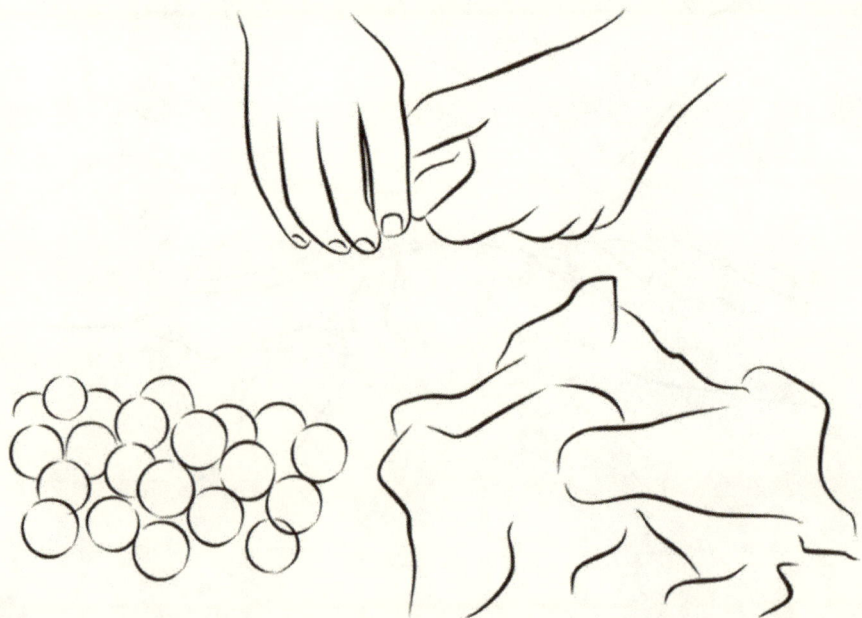

11 **Finished Product:**

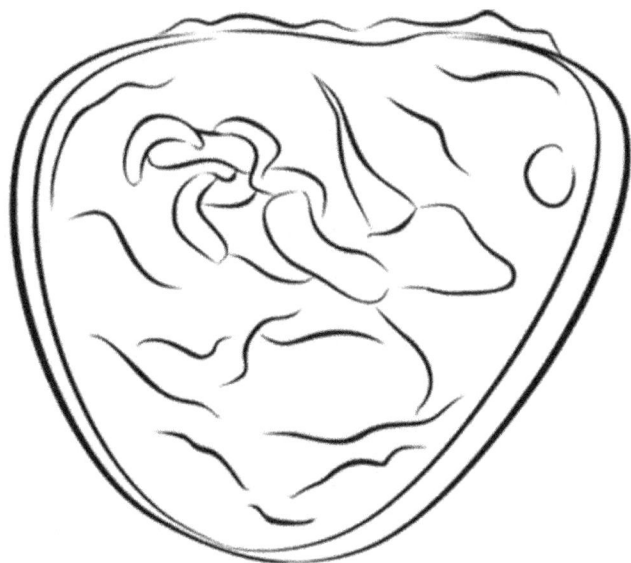

≡ 6 STEP FISH FILLET GUIDE

Filleting a fish that you've caught is simple, and the meat often tastes so much better than anything you can get from a supermarket. There's nothing better than enjoying something that you caught and butchered on your own. Following a few simple steps on how to fillet fish will go a long way. In just six steps, you can have your fish ready to eat.

1 **The first step is to make an incision from the bottom of the gills to the spine.**

2 **Start by removing the head. To do so, place your knife behind the pectoral fin and cut diagonally downward to get through the bone. Repeat this on the other side as well and remove and discard the head.**

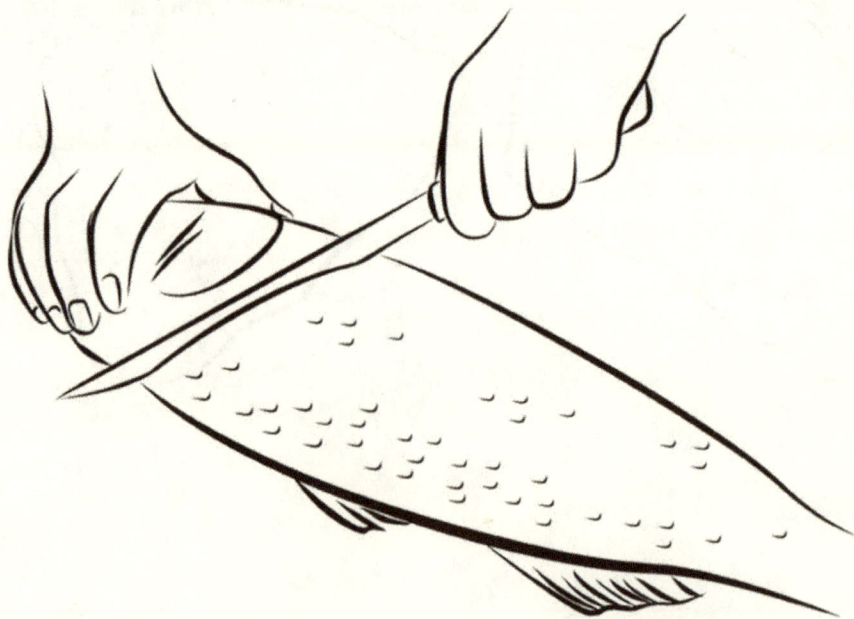

3 Next, remove the tail, using your knife to cut where the tail fin joins the body. Cut straight down through the flesh and bone, then discard the fin.

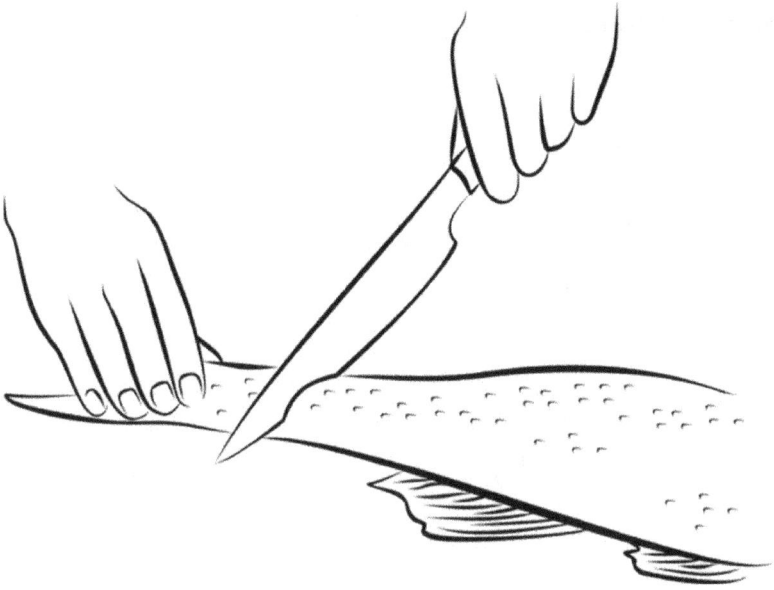

4 Begin at the head end. Use a fillet knife to run along the backbone in as smooth of a motion as possible. It might take over one cut, depending on how large the fish is. You'll want to cut around the ribcage to release the fillet.

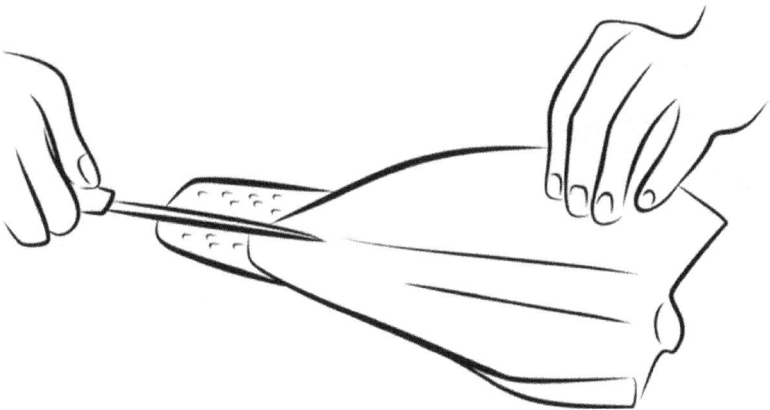

5 Trimming comes next. You'll want to cut the thin belly portion off. While it tastes good and is acceptable, you can enjoy another aspect to cook. You can enjoy another factor that will cook quicker because it is so much thinner. Reserve it to cook separately, or use it for stock instead of cooking it with the fillet.

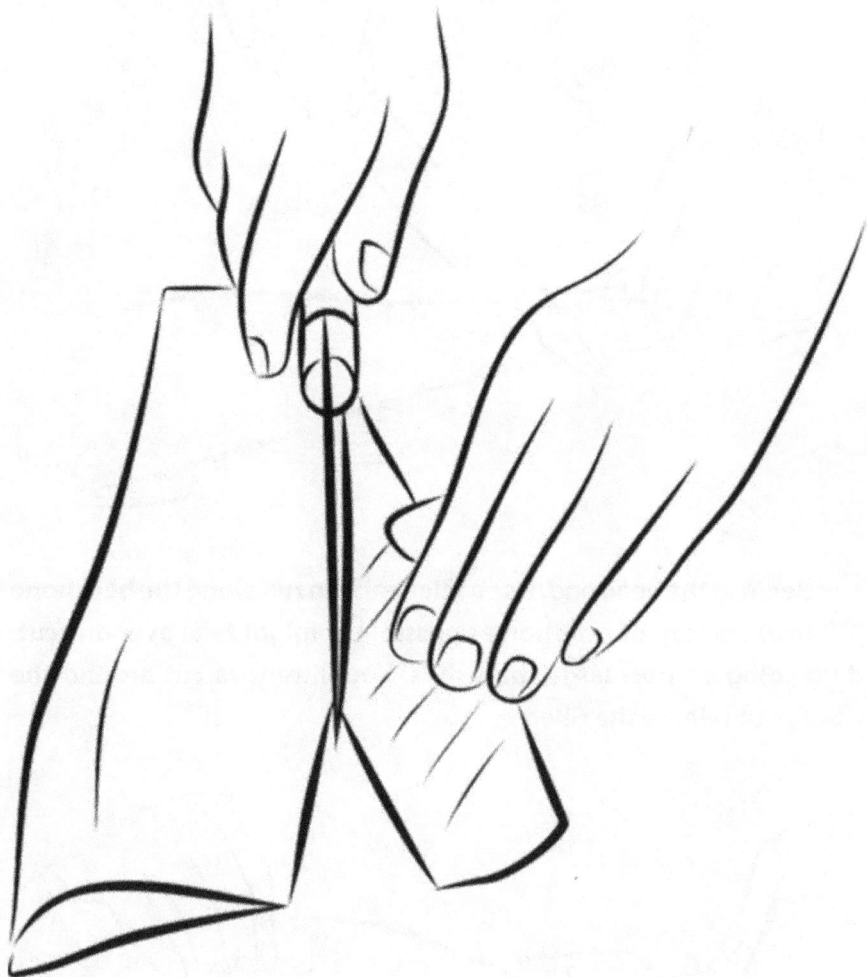

6 Finally, remove the skin. Keep the skin side down, then put your knife at the tail end, situating the blade between the flesh and skin. Use the knife to slowly run along the fillet, tipping the knife downward slightly to avoid cutting into the flesh. The whole fillet should come off and will be ready to cook.

5

SKINNING IS WINNING

While you may hunt primarily to enjoy the food, another aspect that you can enjoy is skinning to mount the hide. Using taxidermy is an excellent way to collect trophies, especially if you have a perfect specimen. Sometimes, an animal can look too good to waste, or you want it as a souvenir.

When you are skinning small game, you need to be mindful of the knife that you choose. Fixed blades that can be sharpened are usually preferred, as they will last longer, but if you're carrying along with a knife as you hunt, you may need to consider getting a folding one. Either way, keep in mind that your blade will need to be small, precise, and extremely sharp. Sharp and precise will ensure that you're able to get the cut in and control it to the best of your ability.

Even if you're just trying to get the skin, it's important to recognize that preparation must happen. You can't usually just leave the animal intact until you can get it to a taxidermist. Instead, field prep as carefully as possible. There are a few essential rules to remember to ensure you have beautiful, intact skins to create beautiful trophies:

1. The carcass still must remain cool. Especially if you are hunting somewhere warm, you want to keep it cool if you're not skinning it immediately.

2. Be delicate with small game and birds. While you might not see the harm in carrying a bird by its neck, you may deform the skin while doing so. You also should not allow dogs to retrieve small game you intend to mount.

3. Cut carefully: always avoid cutting the neck or chest when you do any field dressing beforehand. We'll go over a few simple skinning guides shortly to help you field dress effectively.

4. Ask for tips from your taxidermist. If you have one that you work with exclusively, ask them what they want you to do before bringing the animal to them. Some will have different preferences than others. By acknowledging their preferences before you begin, you up the chances of a successful and beautifully lifelike mount.

As you read over this chapter, you will be introduced to a few key topics. We will go over how to skin squirrels, rabbits, and birds for taxidermy. Then, we will address how to tan hides to prepare them for taxidermy. These topics should provide a cursory introduction to anything that you may need to know for your taxidermy.

HOW TO SKIN SMALL GAME FOR THE FUR

If you want an animal's fur for any reason, whether as a trophy mount, to make other items lined with fur, or for any other reasons, you will need to remove it without damaging it significantly and then treat it. Hence, it's ready to be tanned. Upon removing the skin from an animal, there will still be veins and arteries attached to the skin. There will still be a membrane that you will have to remove as well. We will address skinning squirrels for taxidermy, skinning a rabbit pelt, and skinning birds for trophies. From there, the next section will address how to treat and tan the hide.

SKINNING SQUIRRELS FOR TAXIDERMY

Skinning squirrels for taxidermy differs from the skin for food. Skinning for food is all about getting the skin off completely and quickly to get the rest of the meat ready to cook. Skinning for a mount requires precision and attention to detail that otherwise wouldn't matter. It is crucial that, while skinning, you take your time to be as gentle as possible or you could damage the skin relatively easily. The skin isn't as tough as you might think!

1. **First incision:** The first incision is done at the top with dorsal skinning. This is a favorite for taxidermists as it is a single cut along the spine that requires minimal sewing. Start just behind the shoulders, then cut down to before the hips. Then, you can carefully work the inner membrane along the sides away from the skin with your fingers. If the squirrel is still warm, this is easy.

2. **The hind legs:** To remove the skin from the hind legs, you must work with your fingers to loosen the skin around the hind legs. Push the knee until you can see the joint, then carefully work it down. It should peel off pretty easily. Once you've arrived at the ankle joint, you can use the knife's tip to remove tendons and ligaments connected to the foot bones. Be mindful that tugging too much or cutting a bit too far might destroy the foot's skin. Do so until you get to the toe bones. When you're at the toes, clip the joints connected to the bones, and the skin should detach completely. Repeat this for the other leg.

3. **Stripping the tail:** The tail is especially tricky to remove, but if it tears, you may salvage it by sewing it together, but do the best you can to detach it in one piece. When both hind legs are out, you can grasp the base of the tailbone and the base of the tail skin with your fingers. Then, pull the bone out. Hold the skin in place without pulling it at all as the bones slip out. They should come out in one piece, leaving you with an empty tail. Gently move the hind end of the pelt toward the shoulders.

4. **Skinning the front legs:** Next, work on the front legs. These are skinned, similar to the hind legs. Work the skin off with your fingers to the ankle. Use your knife to loosen tendons and ligaments, and snip at the toe bones.

5. **Skinning the ears:** With the front legs free, you can now start detaching the skin from the head. Pull the skin forward over the neck like removing a shirt, gently continuing until you get to the cartilage of the ears.

You will notice these as little pale lumps on the head. Using your knife as carefully as possible, remove the cartilage, cutting toward the skull to protect the skin. With the ear bases free, you can pull further until you arrive at the back sections of the eyes, which will look like dark, blue areas from underneath the skin.

6. **Skinning the eyes and mouth:** Carefully remove the membrane connecting the corner of the eye to the skull, leaving the eyelids intact on the hide. Do this on the other side and peel the skin until it arrives at the edge of the mouth. Cut the membrane connecting the mouth to the skin and continue peeling to the nose. Use a pair of scissors to cut the nose cartilage away from the skull. The skin is now completely removed.

This process maintains the feet, toes, claws, whiskers, eyelids, and nose, which means it's ready to tan. If you're not ready to tan or take it to a taxidermist, you can turn it right side out and freeze it in a Ziploc bag until you're ready to use it.

SKINNING RABBITS FOR THEIR PELTS

Rabbits are commonly recognized for their beautiful pelts that can be used widely. In this tutorial, you will be left with a pelt that can be lining for hats or gloves or in any other manner you'd like.

1. **Removing the ankles:** Start by slicing around all ankle joints, then twist to break the bone and remove them.
2. **Creating a belly incision:** Carefully, to not penetrate the guts, make a quick slit in the loose belly skin. It helps pinch a piece of skin in the lower abdomen, pull away from the body, and then slit to make an opening.
3. **Loosening skin:** Use a finger to loosen the belly skin from the body. When it is loose enough, insert your knife and extend the incision. Repeat this process into the chest. You should now have a slit from the bottom belly to the chest.

4. **Loosening skin from the body:** Gently using your hands, separate the skin from the sides of the body and the back.

5. **Remove back legs from the skin:** With the skin loosened, be able to slip your finger around the hind leg's knee joint from the inside. Pull the knee inward, and it should slide out of the skin. Repeat on the other leg and loosen the skin around the rear of the rabbit.

6. **Free lower skin:** Detach the skin from the anus, carefully avoiding cutting the skin. Then, pull the skin away from the tail until you can make a clean cut across the tailbone.

7. **Pulling skin from the body:** Holding the skin by the legs, pull the skin up to the neck. Work the skin off of the front legs in the same manner you removed the rear legs. Then pull the skin up and over the head. It should break off, leaving the skin around the head while you have a complete pelt.

SKINNING BIRDS FOR TAXIDERMY

Most birds can be skinned similarly to get a proper hide that you can then mount. Whether you've got a turkey, duck, or quail, there's a good chance that you can use this method to remove the skin to prepare for a taxidermist.

1. **The incision:** Like with a squirrel, you want to create an incision in the back, which can be hidden well and easily sewn up after a taxidermist has finished working on it. The incision on a bird will begin on the back, right before the head begins. Do your best to part feathers to avoid cutting any in half, and try not to get the feathers wet or they will get sticky. The incision should go from the base of the tail to the head.

2. **Separating skin from the body:** The next thing to do is to separate the skin from either side of the body. Peel gently toward the wings. This is easiest if the body is warm. Try to keep the innards and skin wet underneath, careful not to get any water on the feathers.

3. **Separate the skin from the head:** Carefully separate the skin from the rest of the bird, grabbing the neck (not pulling on it). Cut the neck from the body, carefully avoiding cutting the skin. After cutting the neck off from the body, cut off as much of the inner neck as possible.

Use tweezers to pull out the brains and eyes carefully. You have a bird with the skin removed from the body with the neck removed and the head emptied.

4. **Finishing skinning:** Gently remove the skin from around the legs, breaking bones attached to the thighs. You can break the bones off at the thigh, leaving them in the lower part of the foot and the feet. Just make sure there is as little meat as possible left behind.

5. **Skinning the wings:** To remove the wings, break them off where they attach to the body. They will dry out with the skin.

6. **Peeling the skin:** Now, beginning at the neck, you can gently remove the skin, careful to avoid making any holes in it.

7. **Snipping the tail:** The tail will still be attached to the body at this point. You can remove it by carefully snipping off the tail bone, leaving as much meat attached to the body (and away from the skin) as possible. Your skin is now ready to take to a taxidermist.

TANNING SKINS

If you want to tan your pelt yourself, you can do so. If it's a furred animal, you can wash the skin in cold water while finishing the field dressing. This is primarily to keep the skin fresh while removing any leftover fur or blood from the fur. Wash the skin with a mild soap (unnecessary, but can help if you prefer). Get all the blood off the skin. Then, gently squeeze it when you remove it from the water. Don't wring it out, which can stretch or damage the skin. Let the hide dry out overnight. (Tip: Dawn soap is the best. Suitable for cleaning contaminants off of animals too!)

To let it dry well, you can nail the hides to a plank of wood, nailing one corner down at a time. This stretches them out while they drive. Make sure the nails aren't deep; they should pop out with a hammer when pried.

The hides must now be treated for use. There is a layer of the membrane inside of the hide that needs to be removed. It should peel off relatively easily. Try to get as much off as possible. Then, it's time for treatment. A good treatment is a soak in water, salt, and borax.

The hide's inner layer should be coated with a thick layer of salt. This salt should be deep enough to coat the whole thing. Make sure there is no hide left showing through it. This will remove moisture out and cure the hide, so it does not rot. Add more salt every day or two. You can keep the hides nailed down to prevent shrinkage or leave them down flat. They need salt as long as they still have moisture. They should feel completely dry when it's time to work them over.

When they're completely dry, you can start working them over. You will use your hands to blend them until they become pliable. Be gentle during this process. The skin will take some time to be worked through completely. Once the skin has been worked through, it's ready to use for just about anything you'd like.

6

PRACTICAL COOKING AND PREPARING YOUR SMALL GAME

Preparing your meat might be pretty intimidating at first. It's hard to know what to do when you've never done it before. However, the first time is the hardest—and it gets easier every time you do it from there! Eating your harvest is perhaps the most satisfying part of the entire process—you're getting to enjoy something that will be delicious, and you provided it for yourself.

As you read through this chapter, you will get a basic introductory guide to each common small game meat you may have hunted for yourself. We'll go over the most common way to butcher up the meat once it's been skinned and field dressed, how to store it effectively, and some of the basic tips for preparing the food in a tasty manner. This chapter is a precursor to the next chapter, emphasizing several delicious recipes using these different meats to enjoy. As you read this chapter, you'll learn about how these meats taste and what they pair well with, so you can also start thinking of your ways that you may prefer to prepare these meats.

Keep in mind that some of these meats may have gained tastes—if you've grown up eating processed foods and supermarket meat, you may not be accustomed to the gamey taste many of these different meats have. They are earthier or even somewhat iron-like. However, if you gain the taste for it or simply enjoy gaminess already, you will find these highly satisfying. After all, what's more satisfying, than living off the land, as we did before we had civilization? What's more satisfying than getting back to your roots and being self-sustaining? And, what's better than knowing exactly where that meat came from and how it was processed? You don't get these benefits from ordering from the supermarket— you get it from growing or hunting your meat. These are important life skills that are crucial to know in case of an emergency.

☰ SQUIRREL

Butchering Squirrel

Once you have the hair removed, you can remove the head, the feet, and the guts. Save the liver, heart, and kidneys. Then, use a pair of scissors to split the pelvis and remove the anus. Wash well and then break down the squirrel.

Begin by removing the legs. Then, slice down the ribcage to behind the front leg. Cut along the bones toward the neck until the forelegs are free, leaving a skinny collarbone behind. The hind legs can be removed by slicing the meat inside the squirrel's leg, right where it is attached to the body. When you see the ball joint, bend the leg and pop the joint out, then slice the remaining meat and connective tissue to free it. Do so for both legs.

Use the kitchen shears to remove the ribs and save them for stock if you'd like. Use shears or a cleaver to remove the hips and the neck, and you're left with the backstrap. The scraps of meat and skeleton can be used for stock.

Storing Squirrel

Butchered squirrels can be preserved by freezing in a vacuum-sealed bag. The rabbit should be refrigerated for 24-36 hours before freezing until the meat is not rigid. Then, it can be frozen. It may also be pressure canned.

Tips for Cooking Squirrel

Squirrel tastes sweet and nutty, somewhere between chicken and rabbit. To enjoy it, consider braising or slow-cooking it, so it is tender and juicy. It can also be used in most chicken recipes.

RABBIT

Butchering Rabbit

Butchering a rabbit is a little more complicated than butchering a chicken but can be done relatively quickly. When the skin and guts have been removed, you can begin preparing the meat for consumption.

Begin by trimming any sinew or silverskin that's left behind on the carcass. Then, remove the front legs. They aren't attached to the body by bone, so they should come off easily. All you need to do is slide the knife up from underneath, going along the ribs, and then slice through it. Remove any sinew or ligaments from the front legs and set them aside.

Remove the belly next. Carefully cut right along the beginning of the loin, and then cut along the edge of the ribs, filleting the meat off the ribs. Trim any inedible bits off and set the belly strips aside.

Remove the hind legs. These can make up about 40% of the total weight. Begin on the bottom side, gently slicing along the pelvis until you can see the ball and socket joint. Hold either side firmly, bending back to pop the joint out. Then, you finish cutting the meat to free the leg. Do this on both sides.

Remove the loin. Begin by removing the silverskin. There are likely several layers on the back to be removed. Remove the pelvis (it can make broth later). Then, use kitchen shears to cut the ribs off the meat (ribs can go in the broth as well). Remove any more silverskin, then portion the loin into suitable serving sizes.

Storing Rabbit

The rabbit should be frozen if you're not using it within 24 hours of butchering. Store it in the freezer in vacuum-sealed bags for between 9-12 months. It can be thawed in the fridge for 1-2 days before using it.

Tips for Cooking Rabbit

Rabbit meat is like a gamy chicken. It's dryer, with a bit of an earthy taste to it. Removing all the silverskin prevents tough sinew from being present on the meat. Rabbit can be cooked in just about any way you could think of; braised, baked, roasted, and stewed are all perfectly acceptable. You can also bread and fry it.

☰ GROUSE

Grouse is known for its richly red meat with a deep, intense flavor. Ideally, you would have younger birds for quick cooking methods and older birds for slow cooking to tenderize them. To tell, look at the feet. Sharper claws and flexible breast bones typically imply younger birds.

Butchering Grouse

If you have field dressed a grouse by stepping on the wings and pulling the feet, you're left with a breast and wings. From there, you must separate the breast from the bones to prepare them for use. Remember that many places require you to keep a wing on the breast for identification while hunting, so know your local regulations.

When ready to use, twist and pull the wings off.

From there, when it's time to remove the meat from the bone, you can use a kitchen knife to carefully separate the breast from the bone, following the breastbone. Ensure there are no feathers, dirt, or bone left in the meat, and you're ready to cook.

Storing Grouse

Make sure the grouse meat is stored carefully. The best way to do so is to wrap the meat with wax paper and then vacuum seal it in a bag. However, they taste the best fresh.

Tips for Cooking Grouse

Before you begin, always cut out the shot that was used to kill the bird. Also, make sure that any extra feathers are removed. Heavily bloody areas should also be removed. Trussing the bird will help it keep its shape as you cook.

Pair grouse with fruit jelly, some game chips, and gravy. Blackberries and beetroots are common flavors.

≡ PARTRIDGE

Butchering Partridge

If you want to roast a whole partridge, you may not want to separate the breast from the wings in the traditional field dressing method that involves tearing the wings and breast from the bottom. Butchering the partridge for use isn't that difficult on its own, though feather removal may take a while.

Begin by removing the feathers from the body and legs. Then, you will want to remove the head, the wings, and the legs at the natural bend. You can remove the legs well by nicking the bend in the ankle, then twisting and pulling out all the tendons from the leg.

To gut, you can lift the anal vent and make a small incision to fit two fingers in, Carefully scrape out the innards, trying not to burst any guts. Flip over the birds and cut along the neckbone to remove the neck, leaving as much meat as possible.

You can leave a slit in the bottom near the tail, which you can use to keep the legs in place by sticking the bottom of the legs into the hole to keep them tucked in before using a truss to keep them close. Then, it's ready to prepare.

Storing Partridge

It's recommended that to store the partridge well, you wrap it with cling film, then use a vacuum sealer. If you're saving feathered meat, you can wrap it in newspaper first, then cling film, and then vacuum seal. It's usually better to prepare the meat to oven-ready states, remove bloodied meat, and ensure it's ready to go when it's thawed. Try to use it within six months, though it should still be suitable for 12.

Tips for Cooking Partridge

Make sure that you remove any damaged meat, a lead that may be left behind from killing. It's not always possible to have perfectly nice meat when hunting, so don't worry too much if you don't land the kill shot in the head. You can just trim off bloodied pieces, and there's a good chance the meat itself will be fine.

DOVE

Butchering Dove

Dove's breasts are the primary part that is eaten. You can do so easily, removing the wings with a pair of butchering shears. Then, use your thumbs to tear the skin across the breast.

Remove the crop (the pouch with the last meal) from the breast and pull away.

Make snips at the bottom of the breast going up one direction, then the other. You've separated much of the breast from the body. Use your hands to pull off the breast on the bone and trim off the wing joints. You've now got a breast attached to the breastbone, and you can discard the rest.

Wash well to remove blood and feathers. To remove the breast from the breastbone, you can use a knife to cut along the bottom of the breastbone, trimming to the keel but not separating it. Then, work along with the others. The breast is now freed up to the keel, and you can gently detach it from the keel and use it.

Storing Dove

Doves can be stored wrapped in cling film and vacuum sealed. If you don't have a vacuum sealer, you can also use freezer bags with the dove and some water to cover up the meat to prevent freezer burning.

Tips for Cooking Dove

Dove is dry and benefits well from using bacon or some other fatty source to keep some moisture. A great way to prepare them is to wrap them in bacon, stick with a toothpick (or stuff with other ingredients if you want to), and fry up quickly. Keep in mind these breasts are small, so that you may need several for a meal.

☰ PHEASANT

Butchering Pheasant

As a larger bird, the pheasant can offer several pieces of meat that can be enjoyed. You will butcher it predominantly the same way you would butcher a chicken, leaving you with eight cuts of two legs, two thighs, two breasts, and two wings.

Begin by disjointing the legs and thighs from the pheasant by cutting in until you've reached the joint. You can use the knife to loosen the flesh around the joint, then twist and pull it to pop it out of the socket. Do this on both sides.

To separate the breast meat, have the pheasant resting on its back and cut close to the sternum, following down where the breast will meet the wing. Do so on both sides. You should have breasts, wings, and leg quarters at this point.

Now, separate between the leg and thigh. The point will be noticeable because of the fat left there. Use the fat as the guide and cut through the piece.

Storing Pheasant

To store pheasant, butcher it down to the form you would like to use it. Then, store wrapped in cling film and then sealed in vacuum-sealed bags.

Tips for Cooking Pheasant

Pheasant can be used instead of pork, chicken, or turkey. However, keep in mind that they're low in fat. You must prepare them carefully with plenty of low temperatures and extra moisture while covering them up.

Do not cook beyond an internal temperature of 165F for the best results, and let it rest for 5-10 minutes after finishing the meal.

It can be served with everyday sides when roasted, or you can get creative. Make sure you brine or marinate to keep moisture.

☰ QUAIL

Butchering Quail

If you want a whole bird with the skin on it, you can do so. Many people choose to remove the skin, but keeping it can help keep the meat moist. The crispy skin is delicious as well. This process involves first removing the head, then dipping the body in boiling water to scald the feathers and skin. It is done for about 30 seconds, and after, the feathers will come off with gentle rubbing motions. Then, you can start processing the rest of the bird.

Rinse off the bird, bend the leg joints, and cut them off. Use kitchen shears to cut from the tail up either side of the spine, spatchcocking it. This will remove the backbone. Without the spine, be able to pull out the neck. Then, all the insides can be gently scooped out. Clean out the cavity and put the bird in the fridge or use it immediately. You'll have a whole bird that can be roasted and enjoyed.

If you want to harvest without skin, you can skip the scalding step and snip off the head and feet. While running water, get a finger underneath the skin at the neck and slowly peel it from the muscle. Then, cut the bird as if you were keeping the skin on and empty the cavity. Clean it up and prepare it for storage.

Storing Quail

Let the meat sit for 24 hours in the fridge or an ice chest overnight for tenderizing. You can also lightly brine it with a bit of salt to help preserve and flavor the meat. You can use freezer bags to freeze it with a vacuum seal.

Tips for Cooking Quail

Quail is very easy to overcook, which renders the meat dry and tough. It is cooked through when the meat is firm like a chicken breast, with clear juices.

The whole quail can be stuffed and cooked a little longer. Make sure the center is cooked thoroughly before serving.

☰ DUCK

Butchering Duck

Like other birds, you can choose to either skin the duck or scald them to pluck. It depends on if you want the skin to be kept to eat or not. With the skin, the bird will be juicier, and you can save the fat. However, ducks are harder to pluck than other birds.

To remove feathers, scald and pluck.

To skin the bird, begin at the neck and cut under the skin. Slice through the skin underneath where you removed the head, then slice down the belly toward the tail. You should be able to pull the skin, separating with the knife. Work your way around the whole bird. For the wings, you can cut off the ends and skin the other joints. From there, it's time to disembowel the gut.

Cut around the vent without puncturing the bowels. Then starting at the belly, cut from the vent to the ribcage. Then you can get the bird. Remove feet and neck, slicing through ligaments between bones rather than cutting through the bone itself.

Clean out the bird, wash thoroughly, and chill. If you want to butcher further, you can cut down the spine to spatchcock the bird and separate it into quarters or eighths.

Storing Duck

Keep the meat in the fridge for 24 hours, soaking in brine. You can freeze after the 24-hour soak to have a much more tender bird. Dry well, then put the bird in freezer bags.

Tips for Cooking Duck

Duck is easier to crisp when using a whole bird.

Serve duck breast medium rare for best taste.

If serving whole, keep in mind that duck breasts have a thick layer of fat, which needs to render when cooking. You can score the skin with a criss-cross and cook skin-side down to melt fat away. If you don't score and prick the skin, you will have greasy meat.

Duck legs are salted overnight then cooked in duck fat to cook slowly to keep them soft.

☰ TURKEY

Butchering Turkey

Most of the time, people butcher hunted turkeys down to breasts, legs, and wings. It's not practical to often keep turkeys in the entire form, though you could cook it fresh from whole if you wanted to. Butchering a turkey is simple. If you've already cleaned the bird, you can remove the skin and start separating the pieces.

Begin at the breast, using a sharp, flexible blade to get through the meat and take as much as you can. Cut a bit of skin on the breast and tear it open. It will be tough, but you will reveal the breast in doing so. Do this on both sides to expose the whole breast.

Start on the breastbone with a sharp, flexible blade and follow the bone as closely as possible as you work the meat-free. Don't puncture the crop while doing so. Separate the crop from the breast and pull it away, so it doesn't puncture and taint the meat, then finish pulling the breast off. Do so on both sides.

Next, you remove the legs. The leg is already revealed due to skinning the breast. Put a blade in to cut the skin down the leg, all the way to the part where it becomes scaly. Pull it off of the leg, and you'll have a clean leg. At the base of the thigh, be able to see the end of the thigh. Cut carefully to separate the thigh from the body. Then, dislocate the joint, pull it free, and slice if necessary. The leg should come free. Chop the leg between the knee and ankle joint, right where the scales begin. You can keep the spurs if you want. Put a knife to cut the ligaments in the joint, twist, and cut any remaining connective tissue. Do this on both ends.

If you want to keep the wings too, you can pop out the wing joint, pushing it from the body, then cut the wing off. It can be sectioned into the drumette and the wingette, at which point you can start plucking and skinning. This is a lot of work, so weigh if you're interested in doing so.

Storing Turkey

When broken down, the turkey should be vacuum-sealed to keep the meat tasting fresh for a year. Keeping it in pieces is often easier than keeping it whole.

Tips for Cooking Turkey

The leg meat can be tender if cooked well. Be careful not to overcook it or it will dry out.

Wings and drumsticks do well in the crockpot.

The gizzard, liver, and heart can be kept and enjoyed.

Consider saving the bones for stock.

GEESE

Butchering Geese

While you could pluck the goose, it's easier to skin them and be done with it. They have a very thick down that can be difficult to separate. If you want to scald them, you can, adding a bit of dish soap to the water to help penetrate the feathers. You could leave the goose whole, or you could break it up into several pieces.

Remove the goose's head and neck, reserving the neck for use later.

Legs can be removed by cutting along the leg and thigh, following the body's natural shape. Cut all the way, then dislocate the thigh joint and cut the rest of the flesh, holding it in place. Make a slit around where the ligament connects to the drumstick, all the way around. Then use the back of a knife to break the joint just above where the leg meets the ankle and pull. You'll have a clean bone and remove the sinew. Do this on both sides.

Wings can be cut off straight between the joints and cook with the legs.

Remove the wishbone so you can remove the breast. Make an incision on either side of the wishbone, twist, and pull. Then, you can remove the breasts. Cut toward the breastbone at an angle following the bone to free the breast and the bottom wing joint. Do this on both sides, and you've preserved much of the meat.

You can further trim the breast, removing the wing. Then, trim the fat off the breast. Remove any sinew as well.

Storing Geese

Goose can be stored frozen and sealed in a vacuum seal.

Tips for Cooking Geese

Goose is very greasy if you're not careful. Score the fat before cooking to help it render well.

The legs and wings are typically cooked in a confit.

≡ BULLFROG

Butchering Bullfrog

Bullfrogs are butchered during the field dressing process. Remember that to do so, you remove the feet, slice skin around the frogs' waist, then pull the skin off like pants. You can then use shears to chop off the leg.

Storing Bullfrog

Freeze legs in 1-lb packs in vacuum-sealed bags.

Tips for Cooking Bullfrog

Bullfrog should be cooked after soaking it in milk to mellow out the flavor. After soaking them, they can be treated like chicken wings.

≡ SNAPPING TURTLES

Butchering Snapping Turtle

After you've cleaned and skinned a snapping turtle (revisit the field dressing guide to doing so), you can then butcher it up. Doing so is easy. Begin by quartering the limbs. Then, cut off the neck and tail.

Use a knife to cut down the backstrap, trimming them as you go. Remove damaged, fat, or sinew. Then, you can store it in pieces.

Storing Snapping Turtle

To store meat, soak overnight in saltwater first. Then, you can use it or freeze it in vacuum-sealed bags.

Tips for Cooking Snapping Turtle

Snapping turtles can be pressure-cooked to keep the meat tender.

If you don't pressure cook the turtle, consider simmering it to tenderize it. Turtle meat can be tough if not cooked well. It may also be fried.

SECRET RECIPES FOR DELICIOUSNESS

≡ **SQUIRREL RECIPES**

DRUNKEN SQUIRREL AND PUMPKIN DUMPLINGS

Time: 2 hours 45 minutes
Servings: 4

Ingredients

For the dumplings:
- Cooked pureed squash (1 cup)
- Flour (2 ¾ cups)
- Nutmeg (¼ tsp, ground)
- Eggs (2, beaten lightly)
- Ricotta cheese (1 cup)
- Parmesan cheese (¼ cup)
- Salt (a pinch)
- Butter (3 Tbsp.)

For the squirrel
- Butter (3 Tbsp.)
- Squirrel thighs (2 lbs)
- Salt to taste
- Vermouth (1 cup)
- Bay leaves 6
- Squirrel stock (½ cup; can substitute chicken stock if you don't have any)

For the veggies
- Butter (2 Tbsp.)
- Onion (1, sliced)
- Garlic (2 cloves, thin sliced)
- Kale (1 lb., chopped)
- Pecans (½ cup)
- Salt and pepper to taste

Instructions

1. Prepare the squirrel. Set the oven to 325F and use cast iron or other ovenproof pans, melt butter, and browning squirrel legs. They should be nicely browned.
2. When browned, toss in the vermouth to deglaze the pan. Don't forget to scrape the brown parts stuck to the pan. Toss in the stock and bay leaves, put a cover on the pot, and cook in the oven for 2 hours until the meat is tender but not entirely falling off the bone.
3. Prepare the dumplings next. Begin by mixing the ricotta, squash puree, eggs, and parmesan into a bowl. Toss with salt and nutmeg. Then, start adding flour 1 cup at a time. You may need extra to get a nice dough.
4. Prepare a big pot of boiling water. Then, toss in some salt.
5. Roll the dough into a long log that's about as thick as a finger. Then make pieces roughly ¼ inch thick. Wipe the knife as necessary.
6. Place out a baking sheet with flour, then use it to roll each piece of dough into round balls. Flour is key to avoiding sticking.

7. Cook the dumplings in the water in batches, waiting for the dumplings to float and waiting another minute. Take out the dumplings and leave them on an oiled baking sheet.

8. When the squirrel is done cooking, take it to the stovetop. Take another large pan with 3 Tbsp. Butter on medium-high. Put the dumplings in a single layer. Let them sear for a minute and a half to two minutes, letting them brown. Then toss the pan and mix them up for another few minutes to sear more. Take them out, put them in a bowl, and put the bowl in the oven (which should be off and still warm.)

9. Add more butter to the pan if there isn't much left in there. Then, toss in the onions and let them cook for 6-8 minutes. Stir regularly. Then add in the kale, pecans, and garlic, sauteeing for a few minutes to coat everything. Drop the heat down and cover the pan until the kale is wilted.

10. Serve warm and enjoy.

PAPRIKA SQUIRREL STEW

Time: 2 hours, 20 minutes
Servings: 8

Ingredients

- Squirrel (3 whole, cut into serving pieces)
- Salt to taste
- Flour to prevent sticking
- Olive oil (⅓ cup)
- Onions (2 cups, sliced)
- Garlic (3 cloves, minced)
- Tomato paste (1 Tbsp.)
- White wine (1 cup)
- Cider vinegar (¼ cup)
- Oregano (1 tsp)
- Red pepper flakes (½ tsp)
- Paprika (1 Tbsp.)

- Tomatoes (2-3 cups, whole peeled, torn up)
- Smoked sausage (1 lb., kielbasa works well)
- Greens (1 lb., kale, chard, etc.)
- Pepper to taste

Instructions

1. Make sure all pieces of squirrel are butchered down into pieces. Then, salt and coat with a bit of flour. Use some olive oil in a Dutch oven on medium-high heat. Cook the squirrel in single-layer batches without overcrowding the pot. As you do, move browned pieces to the side while finishing the rest.

2. When all pieces are browned and set aside, saute the onion until it browns on the edges. Then, cook in the garlic for another minute. Mix in tomato paste and let it cook for 3 minutes with regular stirring.

3. Toss in white wine, vinegar, and 1 quart of water. Mix the oregano, red pepper, and paprika in. Then mix in the tomatoes and finally, the squirrel. Combine well and simmer it. Cook until the squirrel falls off the bone, roughly 90 minutes. Pull out the squirrel to remove all bones, then toss the meat back into the pot. Salt to taste.

4. Mix in the sausage and greens for another 10 minutes until the greens are done. Mix in salt and pepper if necessary and vinegar to taste and enjoy.

≡ RABBIT RECIPES

RABBIT CURRY

Time: 1 hour
Servings: 4

Ingredients

- Vegetable oil (¼ cup)
- Rabbit meat (2 lbs., removed from the bone and cut in chunks)
- Salt (to taste)
- Yellow onion (2 cups, sliced)
- Ginger (2 Tbsp., minced)
- Garlic (2 Tbsp. minced)
- Tomato puree (1 can, 14 oz.)
- Greek yogurt (1 cup)
- Water (2 cups)
- Bay leaves (2)
- Turmeric (1 tsp)
- Curry powder (2 Tbsp.)
- Garam masala (1 Tbsp.)
- Cilantro (¼ cup, chopped)

Instructions

1. War oil in a large pot on medium-high. Dry the rabbit with a paper towel, then saute until browned. As the meat cooks, season with salt. When they're brown, remove them into a bowl and set them aside.
2. Toss in the onions to the pan and allow them to saute until the edges turn brown. Then, toss in garlic and ginger until fragrant, another minute.
3. Toss the meat back into the pan alongside the tomato, bay leaves, curry powder, turmeric, and water. Mix in the yogurt gently, simmering. Then salt to taste before simmering for 30 minutes.
4. Finish up with garam masala and cilantro, then serve over rice.

ORANGE RABBIT

Time: 2 hours 30 minutes
Servings: 6

Ingredients

- Olive oil (2 Tbsp.)
- Garlic (4 cloves)
- Salt (1 Tbsp.)
- Orange juice (½ cup)
- Rabbit (6 pieces, roughly 2.5 lbs.)
- Red onion (2, thinly sliced)
- Lemon juice (½ cup)

Instructions

1. Combine the oil, garlic, orange juice, and salt in a blender until the garlic is finely minced. Then, put the rabbit into a bowl or bag that can be sealed and marinate it in the mixture for an hour.
2. Preheat the oven to 400 degrees F. Then, move the rabbit to a casserole dish. Cover it up with foil and cook for 15 minutes, then drop the temperature down to 325 F and roast for an hour.
3. Slice up the onion and marinate in lemon juice and salt.
4. Serve the rabbit on a bed of lettuce, topped with the marinated onion slices. Enjoy!

☰ GROUSE RECIPES

SAUTEED GROUSE AND PEACH-BALSAMIC SAUCE

Time: 50 minutes
Servings: 4

Ingredients

- Butter (2 Tbsp.)
- Garlic (2 cloves)
- Grouse (2 birds, cut into quarters)
- White wine (¼ cup)
- Chicken stock (¼ cup)
- Tarragon (2 tsp)
- Peach jam (¼ cup)
- Balsamic vinegar (1 tsp)

Instructions

1. In a large skillet, melt the butter on low, mixing in the garlic. Let it bubble gently for 10 minutes to infuse the garlic into the butter fully. Pull out the garlic and set it aside.
2. Raise the heat to medium-high, then brown the grouse in the butter. It should brown for about 3 minutes per side until golden. Then remove the grouse and set it aside.
3. When the grouse is ready, pour in white wine into the skillet, simmering for 20 seconds, and deglaze the pan. Then, mix in the chicken stock, jam, and tarragon. Let it simmer for 5 minutes on medium-low. Mix in the vinegar and let cook for another 2 minutes.
4. Put the grouse back in the pan with the sauce and finish cooking, another 3-5 minutes.

ROAST GROUSE

Time: 25 minutes
Servings: 2

Ingredients

- Whole grouse (2)
- Butter (10 grams)
- Juniper berries (1 tsp., crushed)
- Thyme (4 sprigs)
- Salt and pepper to taste
- Streaky bacon (4 rashers)

Instructions

1. Set the oven to 400F. Then, season the birds with salt and pepper on the inside and out. Put the berries into the cavities, then place a sprig of thyme underneath each leg. Place two pieces of bacon over the breast of each grouse.

2. Warm butter (or duck fat if you have it) in an ovenproof pan. Sear the birds' backs, then each side until golden brown. Turn them on their backs.

3. Roast for 15-20 minutes, depending on their size. Then let them rest for 5 minutes before serving.

≡ **PARTRIDGE RECIPES**

HERBY ROAST PARTRIDGE

Time: 45 minutes
Servings: 4

Ingredients

- Partridges (4, young and plump)
- Thyme (6 sprigs)
- Juniper berries (12)
- Butter (100g)
- Bacon (8 thin rashers)
- Pears (2)
- Lemon juice (a splash)
- White bread (4 slices)
- Rowan or quince jelly (2 Tbsp.)
- Vermouth (1 glass)

Instructions

1. Make sure all birds are feather-free while the oven preheats to 425F.
2. Remove the leaves from the thyme sprigs, then crush them with the juniper berries, butter, and salt and pepper (to taste) with a mortar and pestle. Keep 1 Tbsp. Aside and use the rest to spread over the birds, focusing on the breasts.
3. Put bacon on a chopping board and stretch them out to thin them without breaking them. Then wrap them over the birds, putting them in a roasting tin.
4. Slice the pears, mixing with a splash of lemon juice. Then, cook in the Tbsp. of herby butter. When they're pale gold, move them to the roasting tin with the partridges. Roast for 20 minutes, then peel the bacon off if it has become crisp. If the birds aren't done, cook for another 10 minutes.

5. Take the bread and cut it into little squares. Warm a bit of butter in the pan used for the pears. Then, fry until the bread becomes crisp and drain well on a paper towel.

6. Pull the tin out of the oven and set birds on fried bread. Place bacon and pear beside them. Put the roasting pan over a medium temperature and mix in the jelly to melt, then add the wine to deglaze the pan. Boil, then use as a gravy.

PARTRIDGE BAKED BEANS

Time: 10 hours
Servings: 8

Ingredients

- Dried great northern beans (2 cups)
- Salt pork (2 oz., cubed in ¼" pieces)
- Dried mustard (1tsp)
- Dark brown sugar (½ cup)
- Molasses (¼ cup)
- Ketchup (2 Tbsp.)
- Salt and pepper
- Partridge (1 whole bird, cut in 6-8 pieces)
- Chicken stock (2 cups)

Instructions

1. Put the beans in a big casserole dish to soak in cold water for 4 hours overnight. Drain them and then put the beans back in the casserole dish with 3 cups of water.

2. Set the oven to 300 degrees F. Put in the pork, mustard, onions, brown sugar, ketchup, and molasses. Season with salt and pepper to taste. Then, bake until beans are tender, up to 5 hours. If they dry out, add more water as necessary.

3. Put partridge in a medium pot with the stock. Cover and cook on medium until the meat falls off the bones, roughly 50-60 minutes. Remove the bones.

4. Combine the partridge with the stock and beans together right before serving.

≡ DOVE RECIPES

Teriyaki Dove

Time: 1 hour, 30 minutes
Servings: 4

Ingredients

- Sake (¼ cup)
- Mirin (¼ cup)
- Rice vinegar (2 Tbsp.)
- Soy sauce (3 Tbsp.)
- Sugar (2 tsp)
- Corn starch (½ tsp to thicken—can be omitted if you don't want a thick sauce)
- Doves (12)
- Vegetable oil (3 Tbsp.)
- Sesame oil
- Sesame seeds for garnish

Instructions

1. Combine the sake, mirin, soy sauce, and sugar in a pot, warming until the sugar dissolves. Then, turn the heat off and let it cool. When cool, bathe the birds in the marinade, breast down for an hour.
2. Put the marinade in a pot and boil to a syrup, or thicken with cornstarch and water. Add vinegar to taste.
3. Heat your grill well, scraping the grates and closing the lids. Use some vegetable oil on a paper towel and a pair of tongs to grease the grill grates, then lightly coat the birds with sesame oil. Place them breast up on the grill with the lid closed for 4 minutes.
4. Open the lid and slather the doves with the reduced marinade. Turn them onto their sides to paint the bottom as well. Grill with the cover opens for another 2 minutes to grill the sides as well.

5. Turn the bird's breast down and paint the bottom with the marinade. Grill another 2-3 minutes with the cover open to brown the skin.

6. Take them off from the heat, coat with marinade sauce, and let cool for 5 minutes. Serve sprinkled with sesame seeds.

DOVE AND CORNBREAD CASSEROLE

Time: 1 hour 30 minutes
Servings: 4

Ingredients

- Dove breast (8)
- Celery (½ cup, chopped)
- Green onion (¼ cup, sliced)
- Parsley (2 Tbsp., fresh)
- Butter (¼ cup)
- Cornbread stuffing mix (3 cups)
- Chicken broth (1 cup)
- Marjoram leaves (½ tsp)
- Salt (½ tsp)
- Pepper (⅛ tsp)

Instructions

1. Set the oven to 350F and grease a casserole dish.

2. In a large pan, saute the onion, celery, and parsley in butter on medium heat. They should become tender.

3. Toss in everything but the dove. Mix well until thoroughly moist. Put half of the stuffing mix in the casserole dish. Then, place the dove breasts over the stuffing. Cover entirely with the rest of the stuffing.

4. Bake without a cover for about an hour until the dove is tender.

≡ PHEASANT RECIPES

PHEASANT PICCATA

Time: 25 minutes
Servings: 5

Ingredients

- Pheasant breasts (10)
- Salt (1 tsp)
- Pepper (1 tsp)
- Flour (⅓ cup)
- Unsalted butter (3 Tbsp.)
- Olive oil (3 Tbsp.)
- Chicken broth (½ cup)
- White wine (½ cup)
- Capers (2 Tbsp.)
- Lemon juice (2 Tbsp.)
- Lemon (1, sliced)

Instructions

1. Season breasts with salt and pepper. Warm 2 Tbsp. Butter and 2 Tbsp. Olive oil over medium heat.
2. When the butter has melted and mixed with oil, dredge each breast in flour for a light coating. Then saute for 3-4 minutes on each side until proper internal temperature has been reached (165 F). Cook in two batches to prevent overcrowding if necessary, keeping the first batch warm in foil while cooking the second batch.
3. When all breasts are cooked, use chicken broth, wine, remaining butter, lemon, and capers to the pan. Mix well to deglaze the bottom of the skillet, scraping well, and simmer for 3 minutes.
4. Serve breasts with a spoonful of buttery lemon sauce drizzled over, with a side of pasta or potatoes.

TANGERINE ROASTED PHEASANT

Time: 2 hours
Servings: 4

Ingredients

- Garlic (1 clove)
- Salt
- Tangerine juice (fresh squeezed, from 2 tangerines)
- Tangerine zest (1 ½ tsp)
- Tangerine (1, halved)
- Tarragon (1 tsp, dried)
- Olive oil (2 Tbsp.)
- Pepper (to taste)
- Carrots (2, halved and cut into 2-inch pieces)
- Potatoes (½ lb, quartered)
- Plum tomatoes (4, ripe, halved, and seeded)
- Pheasant (2 ½ lb)
- Tarragon (2 sprigs)
- Tart apple (½, cored and cut)
- Shallots (2, peeled and halved)
- Sage (3-4 sprigs)
- Turkey bacon (3 slices)
- Chicken broth (⅛ cup)

Instructions

1. Set the oven to 350 F. Mince garlic and mix with salt in a bowl. Mix in the tangerine juice and zest, olive oil, tarragon, and pepper. Set mixture aside.
2. Blanch the potato and carrot for 7 minutes. Then, drain well and set aside in a bowl with tomatoes.
3. Loosen the skin of the pheasants gently, placing a sprig of tarragon on each side. Gently put the skin back in place. Squeeze the tangerine into

the cavity, sprinkling in salt and pepper. Mix in the shallots, apple, and sage into the cavity, and tie the legs with twine.

4. Put veggies in a roasting pan, tossing with the garlic-tangerine mix. Put the pheasant atop veggies, breast up, then brush with some of the tangerine oil. Spread the three pieces of bacon over the breast and pour broth at the bottom of the pan.

5. Roast for an hour, basting every 20 minutes. Remove the bacon and roast another 20-30 minutes until done. Let rest for 10 minutes. Carve and serve.

≡ **QUAIL RECIPES**

TANDOORI QUAIL

Time: 45 minutes
Servings: 4

Ingredients

- Greek yogurt (1 cup plain)
- Lemon juice (2 Tbsp.)
- Lime juice (2 Tbsp.)
- Ginger (1 Tbsp., grated)
- Garlic (2 cloves, grated)
- Paprika (1 Tbsp.)
- Coriander (2 tsp)
- Cumin (2 tsp)
- Turmeric (1 tsp)
- Cilantro (3 Tbsp.)
- Quail (8, halved lengthwise)
- Salt and pepper
- Vegetable oil

Instructions

1. Mix yogurt, lemon and lime juice, ginger, garlic, cilantro, coriander, cumin, turmeric, 2 tsp salt, 1 Tbsp oil in a bowl. Combine well, then transfer to a large resealable bag. Toss in the quail and seal, pressing out air. Refrigerate overnight.
2. Pull out the quail and let it stand for 30 minutes to come to room temperature.
3. Light a grill, oil the grates. Season the quail with salt and pepper. Grill, turning once until meat is barely pink. Transfer to a platter and garnish with cilantro. Serve.

FRIED QUAIL

Time: 20 minutes
Servings: 4

Ingredients

- Quail (8, whole)
- Salt and pepper to taste
- Flour
- Peanut oil

Instructions

1. Rinse quail and pat it dry with paper towels.
2. Season the birds with salt and pepper on the inside and out.
3. Coat the quail in flour to coat thoroughly.
4. Heat 1 inch of oil in a cast-iron skillet to get it hot enough to fry.
5. Put quail in the oil and fry, turning until it's golden brown everywhere.
6. Pull the quail out and let it dry on a paper towel. Serve and enjoy.

≡ **DUCK RECIPES**

ROAST DUCK

Time: 2 hours
Servings: 4

Ingredients

- Ducks (2, go for fat ones)
- Kosher salt (1 Tbsp.)
- Lemon (1, cut in half)
- Rosemary, parsley, or thyme (4 sprigs)

Instructions

1. Set the oven to 325F. Use a needle to prick the skin all over the duck skin, careful not to pierce the meat to release the fat. Don't forget to prick the back and sides.
2. Rub cut lemon all over the ducks, then stick ½ of the lemon in each cavity.
3. Salt the birds liberally, then stuff with the herbs. Let sit at room temperature for 30 minutes.
4. Roast the ducks in a large cast-iron pan, or another ovenproof pan. Start checking at 40 minutes. It could take up to 90 minutes for a large or store-bought duck, depending on size. Pull the duck out and baste it.
5. Boost temperature to 450F. When preheated, put the birds back in the oven. Crisp the skin for 15-20 minutes or until crisp.
6. Let birds rest for 5-10 minutes before serving.

DUCK RAGU

Time: 2 hours 50 minutes
Servings: 4

Ingredients

- Duck legs (2 large)
- Carrot (1, chopped finely)
- Onion (1, chopped finely)
- Celery (1 stalk, chopped finely)
- Orange zest (½ orange peel worth)
- Cinnamon (1 tsp)
- Pureed tomato (1 cup)
- Tomato paste (1 Tbsp.)
- White wine (⅔ cup)
- Chicken stock (5 cups)
- Salt and pepper to taste
- Bay leaf (1)
- Olive oil (2 Tbsp.)
- Pappardelle pasta (14 oz)
- Parmesan cheese to taste

Instructions

1. Season the duck legs with salt and pepper. Then, rub it with ½ tsp cinnamon. Sear the legs in a large pan using a bit of olive oil for 7-8 minutes per side until they're brown. Set them aside.
2. Pour 1 Tbsp. Olive oil into the pan, then saute the carrot, onion, celery, orange zest, bay leaf, and the remainder of the cinnamon. Let it saute for 10 minutes, stirring regularly.
3. Put in the duck, then mix with the wine. Reduce the wine by 50%, then add the juice, pureed tomato, and tomato paste. Stir well, then mix in the stock. Simmer uncovered for 2 hours. If the sauce reduces too much, add more stock.

4. Turn the sauce off and pull out the duck. Let the duck cool for 10 minutes on a cutting board, then shred the meat. Chop, then toss back into the sauce.

5. Prepare the pasta according to instructions, then serve.

TURKEY RECIPES

GRILLED TURKEY BITES

Time: 2 hours 10 minutes
Servings: 6

Ingredients

- Bacon (1 lb, thick-cut)
- Turkey breast (1-1 ½ breast, cubed into 1 ½" pieces)
- Jalapenos (3, sliced in coins)
- Olive oil (¼ cup
- White vinegar (2 Tbsp.)
- Worcestershire sauce (2 Tbsp.)
- Pepper (½ tsp)
- Garlic (2 cloves, minced)
- Salt (1 tsp)
- Brown sugar (1 Tbsp.)

Instructions

1. Mix vinegar, worcestershire sauce, pepper, salt, garlic cloves, and sugar together. Then, marinate the turkey in the mixture for 2 hours.
2. Cut bacon strips in half.
3. Put one jalapeno slice in the center of each piece of bacon and then one cube of turkey on top of the jalapeno. Wrap well, then pin together with a toothpick. Repeat this for all the turkey.
4. Put the grill on medium heat (350 degrees). Put rolls on the sides and cook slowly, turning regularly. Turkey should be done when bacon is fully cooked. Let it rest for 5 minutes and serve.

TURKEY FRIED RICE

Time: 30 minutes
Servings: 4

Ingredients

- Vegetable oil (6 tsp)
- Eggs (2)
- Turkey breast (1 cup, diced)
- Bell pepper (1, chopped)
- Onion (1, chopped)
- Soy sauce (to taste)
- Carrots (2, julienned)
- Cooked rice (2 cups, preferably a day old)
- Broccoli (1 cup, florets)

Instructions

1. Heat a wok with 2 tsp oil. Toss in the veggies and saute until they are tender-crisp.
2. Remove the veggies and set them aside.
3. Add 2 more tsp oil and scramble eggs. Remove the eggs when set and set aside.
4. Toss in the remainder of the oil and cook the turkey breast until done roughly 10 minutes—season to taste with soy sauce. Then toss the veggies and eggs into the wok. Mix well, then toss in the rice and any extra soy sauce if desired. Mix well and serve hot.

GOOSE RECIPES

BBQ PULLED GOOSE

Time: 6 hours
Servings: 8

Ingredients

- Goose breast (2 lb., boneless and skinless)
- Butter (2 Tbsp.)
- Onion (1, chopped)
- Garlic (3 cloves, crushed)
- Worcestershire sauce (¼ cup)
- Chicken stock (2-4 cups as needed)
- Barbecue sauce (to taste)

Instructions

1. Warm butter in a skillet, then brown breast on all sides over medium heat.
2. Move the meat to a slow cooker. Toss in the garlic, onion, Worcestershire sauce, and enough stock that will cover the meat.
3. Simmer for 6-8 hours on low until the meat shreds readily with a fork.
4. Remove the meat and shred.
5. Discard the liquid in the slow cooker. Mix the shredded meat in with your favorite BBQ sauce. Let it warm up and serve on buns.

GOOSE TACOS

Time: 2 hours, 30 minutes
Servings: 4

Ingredients

- Goose breasts (2 large)
- Canola oil (2 Tbsp.)
- Soy sauce (½ cup)

- Lager beer (⅓ cup)
- Black pepper (1 tsp)
- Cayenne powder (1 tsp)
- Garlic powder (1 tsp)

Instructions

1. Butterfly the breasts, then pound them out to a thickness of ¼ inch. Mix soy sauce, beer, and seasonings together, then marinate the duck for 2 hours, up to overnight.
2. When ready to cook, pull the breasts out, dry them off, and lightly oil them. Sear them down on a heavy frying pan, and place a heavyweight or another flat top pan on top of the meat to press it flat while searing. Do this for 3 minutes.
3. Flip the meat and press another 1-3 minutes until done.
4. Remove the meat and rest it for a few minutes. Then, cut thinly against the grain into taco-sized bits. Serve with tortillas and toppings of choice.

≡ **BULLFROG RECIPE**

LOUISIANA FROG LEGS

Time: 2 hours 30 minutes
Servings: 5-8

Ingredients

- Frog legs (20-40)
- Peanut oil
- Buttermilk (1 qt)
- Eggs (2)
- Dijon mustard (4 Tbsp.)
- White flour (3 cups)
- Cornmeal (1 cup)
- Salt and pepper to taste
- Cajun seasoning to taste

Instructions

1. Soak frog legs in buttermilk for an hour. Then, take them out and pat dry.
2. Put the legs in a dry bowl and season with salt and pepper, cajun seasoning, and any hot sauce or worcestershire sauce you may want. Marinate another 30 minutes in the fridge.
3. Pull legs from the fridge and let them drip on a baking rack.
4. Heat 1 inch of peanut oil in a fryer until 375 degrees.
5. Make an egg wash, beating eggs with a splash of water or beer. Then, add in cajun seasoning, garlic powder, salt and pepper, mustard, hot sauce, and worcestershire sauce.
6. Mix two cups of flour and cornmeal in another bowl. Season to taste.
7. Dredge each frog leg in the last of the plain flour, then dip in egg wash, and in seasoned flour/cornmeal mix. Repeat until all legs are ready to fry.
8. Fry for 3 minutes on each side until golden. Enjoy!

☰ SNAPPING TURTLE RECIPE

CREOLE TURTLE SOUP

Time: 3 hours 30 minutes
Servings: 6-8

Ingredients

- Turtle meat (1 ½ lb, boneless or 2 ½ lb bone-in)
- Bay leaves (4)
- Salt
- Flour (1 cup)
- Butter (8 Tbsp.)
- Celery (2 stalks, minced)
- Onion (1 ½ cups, minced)
- Bell pepper (1, green, minced)
- Garlic (4 cloves, minced)
- Crushed tomatoes (1 18oz. can)
- Paprika (1 Tbsp.)
- Worcestershire sauce (3 Tbsp.)
- Sherry (½ cup)
- Parsley (⅓ cup, chopped)
- Hard-Boiled eggs (2, chopped)
- Lemon zest
- Pepper to taste
- Lemon juice (2 Tbsp.)

Instructions

1. Make turtle stock. Put meat in a pot with 8 cups of water, bay leaves, and 1 Tbsp. Salt. Boil and skim the scum. Let simmer until meat is falling off bones, 2-3 hours.
2. Remove meat and pull off bones, then chop. Strain broth, then put it in a pot over low.

3. Take a dutch oven and melt the butter on medium-high. Then, mix in flour to make a roux. It will take 15 minutes.

4. Toss in green pepper, celery, and onion, then cook for 5 minutes. Then, mix in the garlic for another minute. Toss in the chopped turtle meat and combine well.

5. Mix in turtle stock, 1 cup at a time, until the consistency of gravy.

6. Mix in tomatoes, worcestershire sauce, paprika, and cayenne pepper. It should be thinner than gravy.

7. Simmer for 15 minutes until veggies are soft.

8. Top with the sherry, some lemon zest, and the egg. Then, combine well. Serve, using salt, pepper, and lemon juice to taste.

HUNTING FOR GREATNESS COMMUNITY!

COME DISCOVER THE MOST VALUABLE
HUNTING COMMUNITY!

www.facebook.com/groups/www.huntingsecrets

FINAL WORDS

And that, my friend, brings us to the end of this guide. It has covered a wide range of topics on some of the most essential information in hunting small game. From locating and tracking small game to field dressing, skinning, and preparing the food to enjoy, all the information is there for you to use. Whether you're a new hunter or interested, the information provided is crucial if you want to be successful.

And now, you're ready! You've got all the working knowledge to prepare yourself for hunting, prepping, and eating your meat. You are one step closer to self-sufficiency, and you've learned valuable life skills that will take you far. Hunting is one of the most incredible ways to connect to nature, recognizing the beautiful bounties left behind for you, and now, you can enjoy them yourself. Good luck on your hunting journey, and remember this: hunting is about respect. It is about respect for nature, respect for the animal whose meat you will enjoy, and respect for yourself.

Image Credit: Shutterstock.com

OTHER BOOKS YOU'LL LOVE!

BEGINNERS QUICK START INTO THE SPORT WITH EASE

The SIMPLE HUNTING *Guide*

TRACKING, SCOUTING, AND SURVIVAL SKILLS

PAT GATZ

A Special Gift To Our Readers!

Included with your purchase of this book is our Field Dressing Starters Guide. This guide will prepare you with some essential critical tips not to forget when you start field dressing small game. It has a secret golden nugget at the end, too!

Click the link below and let us know which email address to deliver it to.

www.patgatz.com

9 781777 877972